Woodworking

Easy and Affordable Indoor & Outdoor Projects

(A Step-by-step Beginner's Guide to Woodworking and Its Techniques)

Ronald Reyna

I0558228

Published By **Jackson Denver**

Ronald Reyna

*Woodworking: Easy and Affordable Indoor &
Outdoor Projects (A Step-by-step Beginner's Guide
to Woodworking and Its Techniques)*

ISBN   978-1-998927-05-0

Legal & Disclaimer

The information contained in this book is not designed to replace or take the place of any form of medicine or professional medical advice. The information in this book has been provided for educational & entertainment purposes only.

The information contained in this book has been compiled from sources deemed reliable, and it is accurate to the best of the Author's knowledge; however, the Author cannot guarantee its accuracy and validity and cannot be held liable for any errors or omissions. Changes are periodically made to this book. You must consult your doctor or get professional medical advice before using any of the suggested remedies, techniques, or information in this book.

Table Of Contents

Chapter 1: Basics of Woodturning 1

Chapter 2: What To Consider When Picking A Wood Lathe 6

Chapter 3: Other crucial equipment You Use with the Wood Lathe 10

Chapter 4: Safety Measures While Wood Turning 26

Chapter 5: Wood Turning Projects 30

Chapter 6: Safety and Maintenance 152

Chapter 7: Essential Tools for a Beginner 172

Chapter 1: Basics of Woodturning

Let us start with the resource of first know-how what woodturning is.

Basically, woodturning includes the use of system with a purpose to will let you reduce and mould shapes on a piece of timber due to the truth the wooden activates an axis of rotation. You generally use a lathe, which holds and rotates the timber with some handheld device to achieve a few element shapes and designs you need. You have to think about the lathe the identical manner you receive as proper with you studied of the Potter's Wheel.

Woodturning has been spherical for centuries, dating again to the 1300s whilst the Egyptians invented the 2-individual lathe. With this lathe, one man or woman ought to turn the wood the usage of a rope, and a 2d individual might be maintaining a sharp device to reduce the shapes.

This craft has gotten much less difficult over the years from the discovery of hardier turning gadget and the improvement of recent competencies.

As stated earlier, the number one device applied in woodturning is a lathe. It is important to make yourself acquainted with how each detail works, the way to manipulate it, and what to take into account whilst finding out to spend money on a lathe.

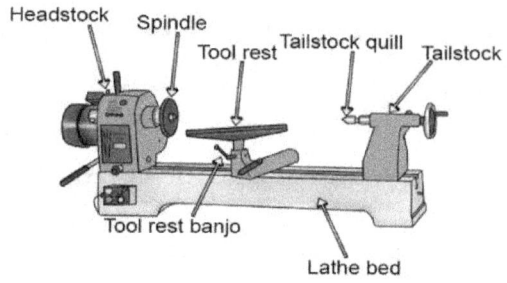

Wood Lathe

A timber lathe is a kind of tool this is made explicitly for smoothing and shaping wood. A wooden lathe should no longer be used for steel works. It has severa factors, and they all artwork collectively to make symmetrical wood items—know-how how every a part of a wood lathe works is essential if any mission ought to gain success.

Parts And Functions of The Wood Lathe

1.Headstock

This holds the fabric being grew to become. It permits switch energy from the motor to the wooden.

2.Spindle

This is in which the only of a type shapes of milling cutters are mounted. The cutters are picked to decide the functions of the final product. The spindle serves because the tool shaft of the headstock and is held in location through bearings on each side, permitting it to rotate at the same time as though stopping it from transferring out of area.

3.Tool Rest Banjo

This detail generally works with the beneficial useful resource of freely sliding alongside the bed of the lathe, permitting you to put your wood in every different manner because it holds the device relaxation. For extra consolation, cutting-edge machines have clamps that hold the banjo in place and can allow quick disengaging whenever for simpler working.

four.Tool relaxation

You area the timber that you may work on proper right here. The tool rest is to be had in several styles and sizes tailor-made for specific operations on the wood. You can alter the peak and bevel to suit as in step with your requirements.

five.Lathe mattress

The bed acts as the "gambling area" that joins the headstock to the tail. It holds all the other factors of the lathe. The mattress offers room for wonderful positioning of the banjo, headstock, and tailstock, as favored.

6.Tailstock quill

The quill comes related to the tailstock, which prevents it from advancing or retracting at the equal time as engaged, making sure that you advantage favored results.

7.Tailstock

The tail stock mimics the movement of the headstock alongside the mattress while jogging on a chunk. The alignment most of the two have to be concentrically set to make certain consistency in the workpiece. It additionally provides greater assist at the equal time as the use of longer or narrow workpieces.

Chapter 2: What To Consider When Picking A Wood Lathe

The following are factors you need to don't forget while choosing your wood lathe:

1.Budget

When looking for a wood lathe, you must recollect the charge, which include all the specific equipment you will need for the venture. This includes grinding tools, wood, and turning device.

2.Size attention

Consider getting a tool as a way to develop with you. Invest in a larger lathe for the purpose that it's going to have you ever included if you need to show large portions within the future whilst nevertheless being useful whilst you want to show smaller ones.

three.Weight

A wooden lathe is sure to vibrate from the turning; consequently, take into account a tool that would face up to the vibration. A heavier lathe works better to useful resource the unbalanced woods.

four.Materials used

Lathes are made from top notch materials, with the maximum not unusual being Cast Iron which goes great to take inside the vibrations.

five.Motor capability

Ensure that the horsepower out of your lathe can take care of your large obligations.

6.Swing capability

The length of wood that you could mount is based totally upon on how extended the gap among the headstock and tail stock stop is. Consider a wood lathe that could accommodate large portions of wood to cover you for destiny projects.

7.Drive and tempo device

You ought to go through in mind a lathe that permits you to modify the charge even as now not having to save you it. Some modern motors have features with a view to allow you to preserve a non-save you pace with out losing any electricity.

8.Headstock features

Some cutting-edge capabilities that would are available in to be had embody:

•Reverse switch, which you could use on the equal time as sanding a bowl down.

•A sliding headstock, that's used at the same time as you wish to exceed the swing functionality of a lathe.

•Remote control, to use in emergencies or to hold a secure distance on the equal time as on the lookout for to forestall the lathe.

•A hand wheel that permits you to despite the truth that flip the lathe on the identical time as not having it on.

9.Banjo and tool rest best

You may also want to paintings with a variety of equipment, so don't forget a tool that may be adaptable sufficient to paintings with numerous equipment.

10. Quality tail stock

Make high-quality that you could adjust the quill freely and smoothly to a massive duration.

Chapter 3: Other crucial equipment You Use with the Wood Lathe

The wood lathe is the primary tool for woodcutters, but it can't feature independently. As a amateur, you need to consider some key subjects at the same time as selecting tools. These consist of;

Long handles – those offer a higher grip and offer greater manage and balance, which allows you create precise designs on the devices.

The fabric being labored on – even as turning timber, you can find out that a few timber might be tougher to paintings with, requiring extra difficult gadget. You will check that it's miles much less tough to artwork on mild woods than hardwoods. Woods like Maple, Walnut, Cherry, Ash, and Rosewood make pinnacle turning substances.

The capability of the device – ensure that your lathe can effortlessly deal with the device to keep away from overworking it, that can in all likelihood break it over the years

Turning operations – There are turning operations, spindle and facelift, which require unique tools. Spindle consists of turning wooden into table and chair legs, baseball bat, while facelift involves the making of bowls, platters, and so forth.

Finish – maintain in thoughts how you need to gather a clean quit or a tough one.

After choosing the ones, you could continue to gain the opposite system, which encompass:

1.Spindle rounding gouge

This is the device to begin with on the equal time as taking walks on spindles for both table legs or lampstands. It has rounded blades to make it less complicated to aspect out the wood piece to the preliminary round shape. They are available awesome sizes, and you can use them counting on your walking undertaking.

2.Spindle gouge

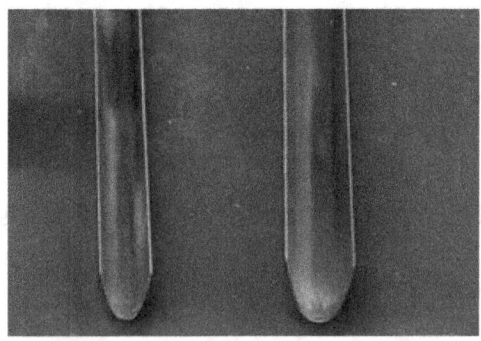

After roughing out your wood right right into a rounder shape, you operate this to feature beads and coves. It has a smaller blade than the roughing tool, which allows for the appearance of more specific records. The spindle is not a hardy tool; for that reason, you want to not use it for extra worrying responsibilities like hollowing out bowls.

3.Bowl gouge

A big manage and a deeper reduce oval at the blade, which allows for chipping, characterize this tool. You can use it for the extra difficult obligations, which grow to be less complicated because of the prolonged address that offers extra benefits on the identical time as turning the timber. You can use it on the identical time as making bowls.

To get the exceptional consequences from the device, you need to apprehend the techniques concerned. These embody;

Pull reduce technique – You will want to keep the bevel at a parallel feature with the wood ground. The approach takes advantage of the bevel to get a purifier ground. Cutters remember it a more superior method because of the reality in location of using the top of the gouge, it uses the out of doors of the quit and the facet additives, making the turning method faster.

Push lessen approach – This furthermore includes riding the bevel, however in comparison to the pull technique, this calls an amazing manner to push your weight in the direction of the tool while reducing. It fine involves using the top on the identical time as the use of the hand to anchor the tool from slipping.

Scraping lessen method – You do no longer use the bevel for this technique; alternatively, use the device's sharp location to scrape out the substances. The gouge is type of located horizontally, with the decrease part of the wing fine touching the timber surface. You can use this technique when the form of the bowl needs adjustment.

Shear scraping lessen – You nevertheless will now not be the usage of the bevel for this technique. Instead, the gouge is held at an nearly forty five ranges angle, allowing the decrease wings to act like shears shaving away thin layers. It may be a hard approach however as quickly as mastered may be very powerful at smoothening such that no sandpaper is wanted at the surrender.

4.Chisels

This can be used for spindles and bowls. You can outcomes strain the device into the wooden to shape it, re-shape it or curve out materials off it due to its blade characteristic on the surrender. When used correctly, it can make unique cuts in contrast to other gear. The blades on the tool are to be had in one-of-a-type inches.

As a beginner, you may begin with a 1-inch, ¾ inch, ½ inch, and ¼ inch. It is nice to note that the device can be tough to apply as a amateur, but you could with out problems draw close it with enough exercise.

five.Parting system

You use this tool even as you need to separate part of wood from the cloth you're strolling on. You may also even out the segments using other equipment.

Furthermore, you could use it to mark thin traces at the piece you're working on. They are to be had superb shapes, at the aspect of diamond, rectangle, and rectangular, so that it will will will let you create specific designs.

You can use this device whilst strolling on spindles.

6.Scrapers

Scrapers are to be had in precise shapes, but most woodcutters use the round nostril and the square nose. You want to apply the round nostril for the internal additives of the bowl and the rectangular one for the outside element. It allows even out the ground, putting off marks left at the back of via the alternative equipment.

7.CBN Grinding Wheels

Due to the friction of rubbing the equipment inside the direction of the wooden, the device emerge as blunt proper away; this makes operating with them very hard. It is wonderful to invest in a sharpener due to the fact you will need to hold sharpening the tool every thirty mins or maybe a lot a lot less. While you are deciding on which sharpener to apply, make sure it does no longer alternate the diameter of your equipment.

eight.Pull noticed

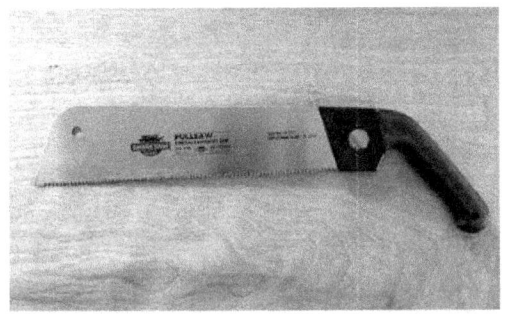

You may additionally moreover need to reduce out quantities from locks of timber before beginning to art work on them. The period relies upon on how large you want your clean piece to be.

nine.Woodchuck

This is established to the lathe, then a tenon is created on the piece of wood and then inserted into the chuck, which holds it in feature as you switch the clean.

10. Jacobs Chuck

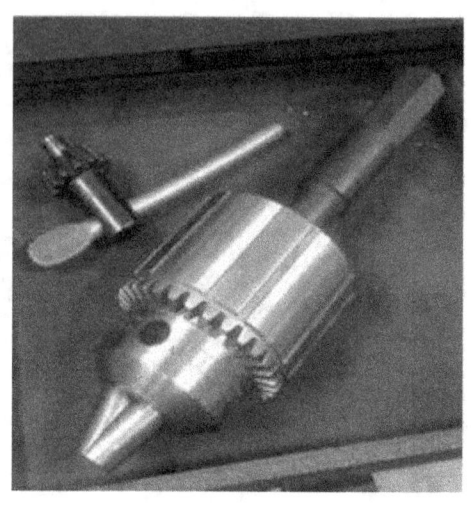

The chuck has a segment in which one in each of a kind drill bits can be delivered to create dips in the wooden as you turn.

eleven. Live Center

This is mounted onto the lathe's tail stock even as centered at the wood block to offer resource as you are woodturning. The stay middle rotates freely due to the fact the lathe runs. This permits reduce friction, which could ultimately reason burnings on wood.

12. Spur Drive

The spur strain is positioned within the headstock and targeted on the easy piece of wooden all through the turning manner, which allows to stress the timber piece.

13. Lathe Face Plate

This is used to beneficial useful resource in the turning of huge devices like bowls. Screws are used to attach it to the wooden piece.

14. Sand paper

After you have finished walking on your task, a few additives do no longer reap an tremendous give up. Here, you operate sandpaper to smoothen the factors. It may be quite a challenge, but it however gets the interest performed. As a newbie, you need to continually sand alongside the wood grain for a smoother forestall.

Do not address the sandpaper at the side of your naked fingers because of the reality you can damage yourself from the friction produced.

15. Paints and finishes

After completing your masterpiece, you may need to complete it by way of along with a expert look to it. Some decided directly to shade their portions, whilst others choose to preserve that woody tone. Understanding the precise types of paint let you in making this choice.

They are;

Oil-primarily based definitely paints – you may use the ones paints whilst you need to gain a swish or matte finish for your project. While the usage of this paint, make sure you decide each proper away on the wood or over a primer specifically supposed for oil paints. Oil paints are greater difficult to smooth up, so try to be unique while portray.

 Latex paint – you could without issue smooth up this paint the use of water and soap; because of this that it is a great deal a great deal much less long lasting and does not provide that an entire lot of a seamless prevent. Applying multiple layers can help cowl brush strokes.

Water-primarily based completely paint – those paints dry proper away and are very safe to use thinking about that they do not produce poisonous fumes. The coloration achieved can stand the test of time. With this paint, pretreatment of wood isn't essential.

Acrylic paint – These can be fun paints to use considering they will assist you to create your very very personal colours. When you need to accumulate laptop pix like an ombre colour, you could aggregate your desired hues and achieve this. They are also odorless and dry in no time.

Chapter 4: Safety Measures While Wood Turning

It is terrific to recognize a few easy safety measures to keep away from any mishaps:

Ensure that the system are sharp – Every woodturner ought as a way to sharpen their tools in advance than starting the approach. It is amazing to sharpen them on a device grinder to preserve the bevel on each tool. A sharpened tool way tons less try to your factor and provides a purifier lessen in your completed portions.

It is likewise much more likely for a stupid tool to loosen up, that may cause an twist of destiny.

Wear defensive gadget – While handling the uncooked wooden, bits of timber can effortlessly fly off and damage you. A face defend is a in reality perfect object to protect the face.

It may want to additionally be first-class to consider carrying rubber boots or leather-primarily based boots to shield your ft from shavings from the wooden. Since that is a hands-on hobby, it is also acceptable to guard your hands thru wearing going for walks gloves.

Ensure there is straightforward air – wooden dust can with out issues discover its way on your lungs, which can bring on some of fitness problems. To avoid this, artwork in an open area or ensure that your protecting device has a remarkable clear out to clean out the air you are inhaling.

Power precautions – every now and then, you may need to change up the system you are the use of, every the blade or bit. Ensure that you lessen the strength first to avoid hurting your self.

To don't forget this, try to use one extension cord for all of the plugs so you will ought to hold alternating as you skip, consequently forcing you to replace it off.

Right clothes – avoid carrying dishevelled clothes as they may results be stuck by way of the machine whilst cutting. Also, avoid carrying any dangling metals like chains and bracelets.

Hand proximity to the blades – motels of pieces of wooden at the blades even as working may be very not unusual. You can also want to, at instances, be tempted to gain in and do away with the bits, main to accidents. The brilliant manner to cope with this is to attend till the blades prevent turning, then, using a piece of wood, push it out. This is due to the truth the blades have to despite the fact that be warm, and you can get burnt.

Ways to paintings with the cutter – at the same time as you're operating, make sure which you circulate the wooden piece in competition to the motion of the timber cutting device. Still on that, typically reduce with the grain. This method that you have to commonly art work from the edge to the center and no longer the other way round, which gives you greater manage over the piece.

Avoid distractions – Ensure which you have your eyes set on the slicing tool when the motor is strolling. A moderate distraction may be a recipe for disaster. Ensure that earlier than putting the device down, you acquire a stable quit instead of dwelling it midway, resulting in a exceptional stop.

Splintering of wooden – to save you splintering of wooden, you can use covering tape to cowl the location you are slicing alongside, which offers a grip for the reducing device and stops splinters.

Next up, allow's have a take a look at the initiatives.

Chapter 5: Wood Turning Projects

Bowls

Materials Needed

Compass and pencil

Bowl gouge

Parting tool

Block of wooden or tree stump

Sandpaper

Drill and drill bit

Furnish

Faceplate screws

Straight facet

Four jaw woodchuck

How to Make a Bowl

Start with the aid of using putting in the wooden block. You can use both a small tree stump or a block of timber.

While using a block of wooden, you'll need to mark out its center. Use the without delay element to draw traces throughout the block, tracing the middle to wherein they meet.

Take your compass and pencil and draw a circle at the block, positioning it getting ready to intersection of the traces. Ensure that the circle fits on the lathe with the beneficial useful resource of seeking to in shape it on, to realise how lots to trim out.

Trim out the edges at the blank piece, which facilitates reduce turning time.

To mount the clean piece onto the lathe, you may want to use a faceplate since it gives a less assailable hold.

To mount it on, make sure you've got were given screws meant for the precise faceplate.

Position it at the center in advance marked out. Tighten the screws the use of the drill bit. Start with the number one screw, however do no longer absolutely tighten it. This permits for wiggle room as you pass at some stage in the faceplate. To collect a degree connection, drill the screws on alternating additives, then subsequently screw down the primary screw.

Attach the faceplate to the lathe through the headstock. Turn it across the headstocks spindle until it sits perfectly. Position the banjo at a 90-degree perspective to the lathe, pulling the device rest closer to the easy wood.

Ensure that not anything sits at the device rest due to the fact this will gradual down the turning due to steady rubbing toward every precise. Ensure that the device relaxation stays parallel to the side of the smooth; this can assist feature the running gear.

Before turning the lathe on, confirm that the timber turns freely with out rubbing on the device rest. Adjust the tail inventory upwards, then growth it toward the easy wooden. Once they may be in contact, lock the tail inventory in

region.

Before beginning the lathe, ensure you have got your safety device on and begin turning slowly. The purpose is to acquire a round form, for you to make turning less complex.

After sharpening your bowl gouge, area it on the tool rest, adjusting it sufficient to the point in which the blade is in keeping with the center of the block.

Ensure you are in a feature without hassle available to the controls.

Slowly start the lathe, growing its pace as you bypass; for a guiding principle, try not to exceed 800RPMS. Unlike taking walks on spindles, bowl turning requires a slower tempo to assist in precision because of the bigger diameter.

Position the bowl gouge on your opposite facet, being cautious not to the touch the turning wood.

Since the bowl gouge is already set in place, use the bevel to align the side of the bowl smooth parallel to the gouge. The bevel will make certain consistency inside the cuts made.

With the bevel in region, barely touch the threshold of the device rest to make a slight skip. Parts of the timber must start shaving off. Switch the bevel to the alternative issue to acquire the same. Keep alternating between the left and the proper difficulty.

Keep smoothening it out till you advantage a wonderfully round form.

When seeking to make smooth cuts, popularity on the usage of the frame and no longer the palms. Any slight alternate of hand role can create debts or traces on regions you probably did not intend to.

Place your left thumb over the gouge's pinnacle, keeping the hand behind the device relaxation. Move your frame forward with out moving the hand characteristic, with the alternative fingers appearing as a guide.

Ensure the proper hand firmly holds the bowl gouges deal with, retaining a parallel route the various bevel and the route you need to cut.

As you cut, make certain you preserve repositioning the bevel parallel to the desired lessen after which lock it in area.

While making this lessen, strive leaning in for additonal stability through the usage of the rush lessen approach with out moving the hands.

To art work on the opposite part of the bowl, flip off the lathe first and reposition the banjo and tool rest at the aspect no longer worked on.

Be eager to hold the identical parallel path, as finished in advance, on the alignment of the banjo and the bowl easy.

The subsequent element calls for you to smoothen out the lowest of the bowl.

Unlike in advance, the gouge will now be pointing away from the bowl easy; maintain doing this until you get a easy give up.

Next, you need to create a mortise, which makes it a great deal less complicated to paintings on the bowl's indoors. Grab the four jaw chuck and close to up the jaws simply. In order to seize the plank nicely, the jaws will need to open up at the identical time as within the joint you may have created.

So, take the measurements of the closed jaws and then add about ¼ of an inch. Transfer this era to the middle of the wooden piece.

Using a pencil, draw a circle at the wood piece to offer a better view of in which you may vicinity the jaws.

To lessen out the mortise, you may need to apply a parting tool as a scraper. Switch the lath on and ensure you hold the tool for the duration of the circle drawn out as you scrap. Ensure that you do not scrape too deep because the jaws will now not art work nicely to

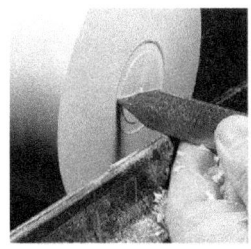

grip.

Smoothen out the indoors of the mortise to provide a higher grip for it.

Try fitting the jaws in and if it goals a chunk tweaking, preserve scrapping the substances off. You can use a skew chisel to scrap out more chunks.

To turn the bowl's outdoors, you want to prevent positioning the gadget parallel to the woodchuck and start placing them in a manner that they may be parallel to the bowl being created.

Start by means of way of moving the device relaxation to the the front of the wood and for your left. Place your device in a way that, whilst turning, it actions parallel to the shape being created in place of wherein it modified into shifting parallel to the bite.

Using the push lessen approach, paintings from proper to left, positioning your self inside the center at the side of your left hand guiding you as you steer collectively with your proper.

Make effective that the position made via the bowl gouge and the flute is pointing some distance from you. As you start, you could make small straight away cuts but curve it to obtain the desired shape with every nearing pass to the curve of the bowl's exterior.

Maintain your hand position and simplest lean to shift your body weight in advance.

As you figure, keep repositioning the tool to rest closer to the bowl to keep away from losing manipulate of the bowl gouge, but usually don't forget to reveal the lathe off.

While turning the out of doors, leave a piece of cloth throughout the base, in which you could function the mortise to offer room for pressure buildup, which prevents the complete bowl from breaking apart.

Keep polishing your system to get smoother finishes.

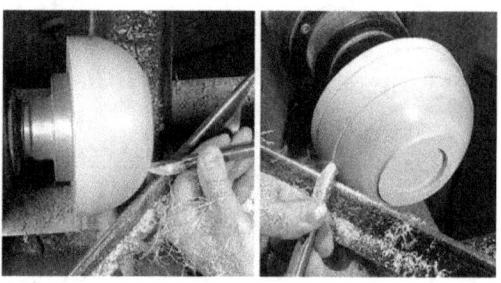

You will want to remove the faceplate to artwork at the indoors considering the fact that its method is now finished.

Next, thread the 4 jaw chuck onto the headstock spindle, positioning it inside the course of the bottom of the headstock.

Expand the jaws of the chew until they healthy snugly inside the mortise. Twist it round to tighten the jaws of the chuck farther.

Turn the lathe on and study if the bowl turns in the function required.

Ensure that you don't over-tighten the chuck due to the fact this may make the turning device difficult.

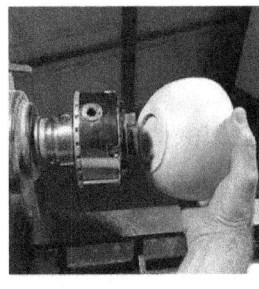

Just as you smoothed out the exterior, start doing the equal. Use push cuts after positioning the bowl gouge on the centerline of the bowl.

The tool rest ought to stay parallel to the front edge of the bowl.

Try and keep a slower velocity of about 1000MPS for the reason that that is a small bowl.

Note that the speed of the lathe need to be inversely proportional to the size of the bowl being grew to become.

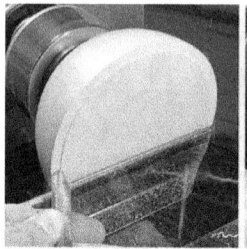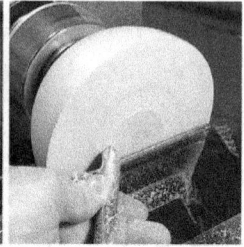

Next, begin clearing out the indoors of the bowl. Without transferring the tool rest, make small passes to remove the fabric.

With the proper hand acting as a manual, bypass from right to left, removing small bits off.

Make a small trough on the brink of the rim via manner of disposing of bits of fabric from it over numerous passes.

With that during place, begin strolling on the interior a part of the bowl.

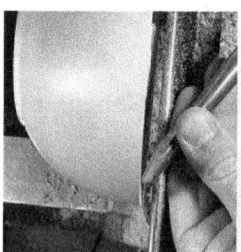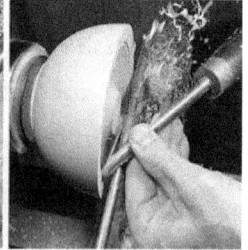

As you work, preserve the middle piece in location as it enables keep it from breaking off and offers a smoother turn.

To maintain a uniform thickness of the partitions, goal to acquire the identical shape as that of the outdoor.

As you turn, ensure that the gouge does now not hit the middle considering the reality that this could avoid the turning way.

To efficaciously form the indoors, feature the bowl gouge at 90 levels and on the 3 o'clock mark and begin turning the bowl using push cuts.

Since the center is packed with waste substances, you can attempt the use of the sweeping curve cuts to fasten the tool.

With every bypass, keep smoothening the indoors and keep phrase of the shape being fashioned.

Ensure which you keep the identical thickness on the lowest as is at the partitions with the resource of no longer removing too much cloth.

Use your arms to check this, making sure that the lathe is grew to grow to be off on every test.

When performed, smoothen out the indoors.

At this point, your bowl is ready to be sanded down. You can use hand sandpaper with the lathe strolling slower, or choose to have it off. After sanding it down, look at a coat of supply to protect the wood and moreover offer it a graceful stop.

Here you could select out to both use oil or beeswax. Make positive to apply a thin layer of it.

If the bowl is supposed for eating, make certain that the give up is solid for consumption.

Leave it outdoor for about an afternoon to dry out, and then customise the lowest of your bowl as preferred.

Unique Wooden Cup

Materials desired

Woodchuck

Chainsaw

Bandsaw

Four jaw chuck

Finish

Sandpaper

Drill bits

Wood glue

Template of cup deal with

Painter's tape

Scrapping tool

How to Make a wood cup

Start with the aid of manner of making organized the woodchuck to make it an awful lot less tough to expose it.

We want to use the middle part of the wooden for this venture, for the reason that it's far a great deal much less chunky.

Take the chainsaw and begin trimming down the edges of the timber to make it a great deal much less tough for the bandsaw to smoothen it out.

Start through smoothening out one component of the timber the usage of the chainsaw. This gives a reference issue while on foot with the bandsaw.

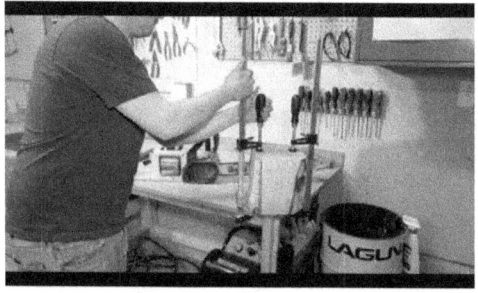

Next, placed it thru the bandsaw ad smoothen out the edges to make it less complicated to

healthy it at the lathe.

On the smoothened-out piece of wood, mark out wherein you would really like the cup to come out of, then trim out the greater.

Mount the trimmed piece onto the timber lathe.

Next, turn the motor on and begin turning the outdoor a part of the wood. Keep turning until you get a spherical shape.

Cut out a tendon on one of the faces of the smooth, and on it, be a part of the 4 jaw chuck to constant it in vicinity as you parent at the indoors of the cup. The tendon reduce out will function the bottom of the cup.

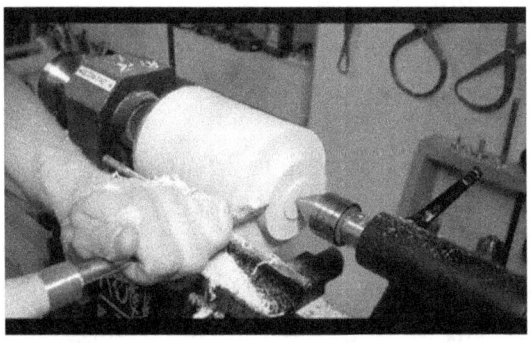

Keep turning the outside a part of the wood whilst smoothening it out.

To hollow out the easy timber, upload a drill bit o the tail inventory, and as it drills through the wood, hold smoothening out the outside element.

After you have made a shallow hollow inside the wood, trade the drill bit into a bigger Forster drill to assist get rid of the relaxation of the materials.

Keep drilling till the cup is in reality hollowed out and use the scraping tool.

Maintain the equal thickness all around the cup to keep away from it from cracking up.

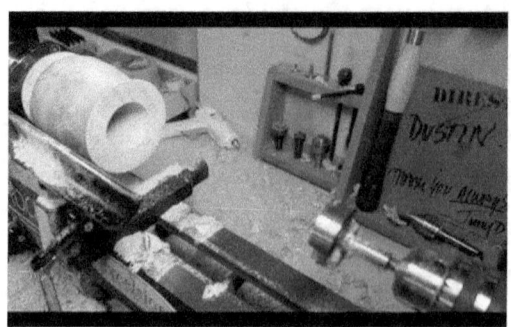

Now that the cup is performed, you need to sand it down for a smoother prevent.

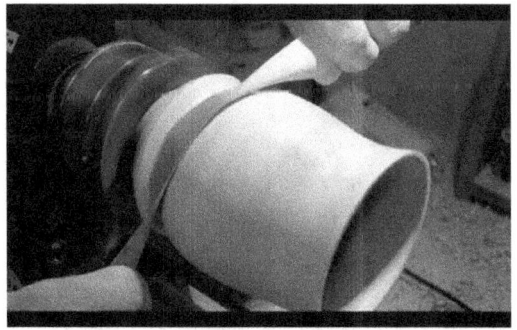

After sanding it down, you may pick out to depart it like that or add a cope with on it.

To upload a control, take a bit of wood and decrease it into half of within the center.

Take every different piece of wood that is barely longer than the alternative and glue the

3 components collectively with the longer element within the middle.

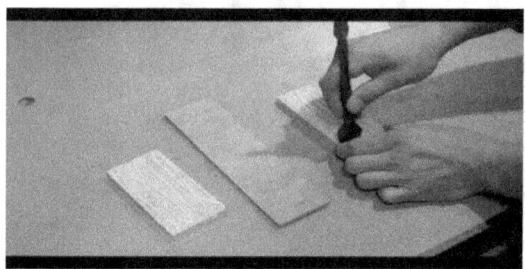

For extra electricity, pick out out a wood that is going within the route of the grain.

After gluing the timber collectively, trim off any extra additives.

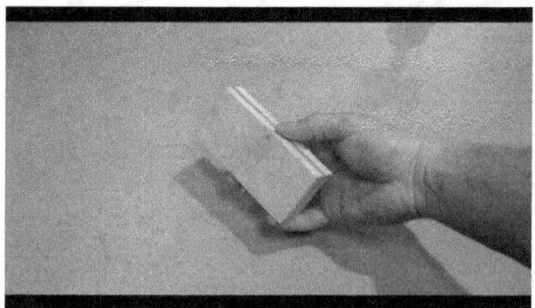

Take the painter's tape and lay it on the block of wood. Glue the template on top of it. This makes it simpler to do away with it at the same time as you're completed.

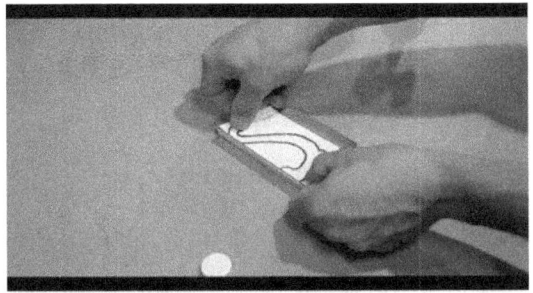

Trim down the timber piece till you bought the supposed shape of the contend with.

As you get in the route of the shape, you may tape the stencil and art work on smoothing the deal with similarly.

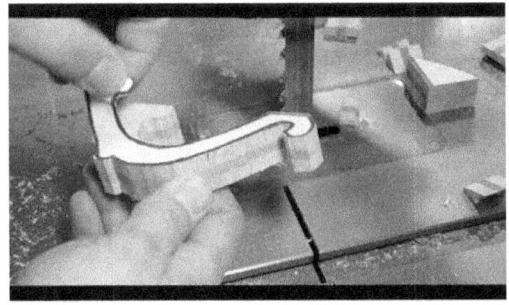

Now that the deal with is ready, take the cup and glue it on.

Start by means of tracing in that you would like the address to move at the cup, after which sand down the a part of touch to make it much less tough for the glue to adhere. Make sure to use water-resistant glue due to the fact the cup can be in everyday contact with water.

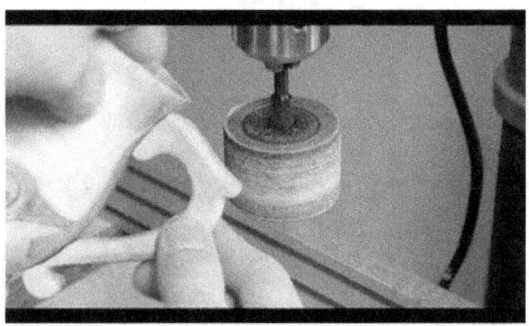

Once carried out, exercise a coat of stop to deliver the wood back to existence, and there, your cup is completed.

Baseball Bat

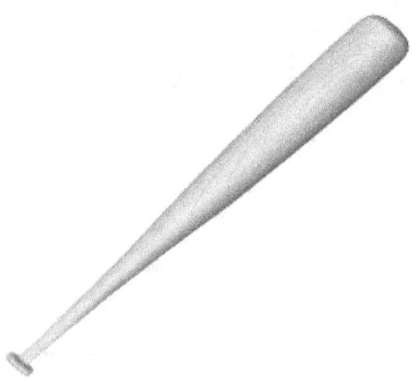

Materials Needed

36" timber bat clean, preferably from Ashwood

Roughing gouge

Skew chisel

Gouge chisel

Pencil

Sandpaper

Varnish end

Wood noticed

Square

Measuring Tape

Calipers

How to Make a Baseball Bat

Start through measuring the middle of the timber, then mark it out with a pencil.

Position it at the wood lathe between the headstock and tail inventory.

Typically, a baseball bat has tremendous diameters on it. The chart beneath will let you discern out the diameters.

Serial

Bat Part

Length

Diameter

1

Knob

zero''

2''

2

Grip

four''

1''

three

Grip

eight''

1''

  4

Grip

12''

1.One hundred twenty 5''

  five

Taper

16''

1.25"

  6

Taper

20"

1.Seventy five''

  7

Barrel

24''

2.19"

 8

Barrel

28"

2.Forty 5''

 nine

End

34''

2.Five"

The diameter changes after every four'', so collectively with your pencil, mark this out to

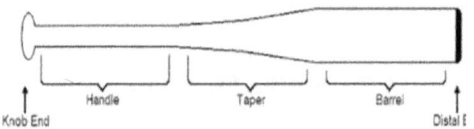

paintings as a guide. Use the calipers to degree the diameters you'll need.

Ensure that the wood clean is cylindrical and if no longer, flip it on the lathe till the shape is completed.

With the device relaxation in region, activate the lathe and start roughing out the timber the use of a roughing gouge.

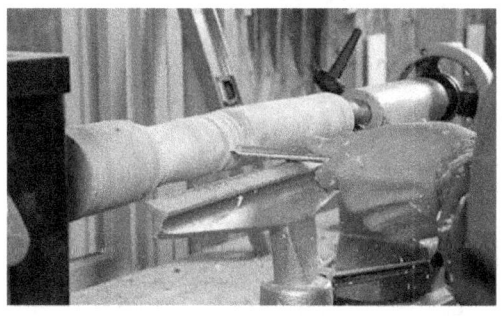

Place the gouge softly at the pencil mark, maintaining the lathe on. Make first-class now not to dig too deep to keep away from going beyond the mark.

Starting with the barrel, use the gouge to do away with extra materials from the wooden as you pass within the direction of the alternative give up. Remember to maintain measuring as you go to keep running at the marked-out components.

As you flow into to the taper, the thickest issue, use the skew chisel to even it out at the same time as continuously using the calipers to ensure the diameter is maintained.

To artwork on the knob and gripper, you can need to decrease the price because of their smaller diameter, to approximately a half of the rate.

For this detail, the gouge chisel will paintings amazing to shave out the timber.

As for the knob, to get an appropriate round form, a mixture of the skew chisel, roughing gouge, and parting equipment need to be used. Keep in mind to keep the fee at a decrease price.

When completed, degree the diameter once more to ensure it's far properly-balanced inside the direction of for a higher swing.

Using the sandpaper, smooth it down for a better stop.

After you're glad with the bat, exercise a skinny layer of varnish or oil to shield the wood for extra sturdiness.

Candleholders

Materials Needed

Piece of timber 5'' x5'' x3''

Bowl gouge

Candle

superglue

Bandsaw

Drive center

parting device

Scroll chuck

Sandpaper

Oil for completing

How to Make a Candleholder

Starting off with the clean piece of timber, mark the circumference of the candle and its middle. This works as a guide whilst you start turning the wooden. The length of the wooden will determine the size of the candleholder.

After marking it out, use the bandsaw to cast off the areas outside the circle made. Getting rid of these corners reduces the time spent turning the wooden piece.

To mount the timber piece at the headstock, use a stress center, putting it inside the center of the circle as you had marked out in advance to offer a less attackable keep as you decide at the candleholder.

After mounting the smooth on the wooden lathe, flip it on and start rounding it off using the bowl gouge. Ensure that the gouge is sharp even as working on the challenge. The first step is to paintings on the outdoors before beginning with the indoors of the bowl.

Using a parting tool, create a tenon on one detail of the clean. This can be used to connect a scroll chuck to mount it on the lathe to paintings at the rest of the bowl.

After growing the tenon, unmount the blank and join the scroll chuck to the lathe. Reattach the clean with the aid of gripping the tenon with the scroll chuck.

Start shaping out the outdoors part of the bowl using a bowl gouge. Use the push lessen approach for purifier cuts.

As you're strolling at the top exterior part of the candle, the usage of a parting tool, start hollowing out the smooth. As you parent, ensure the diameter of the recess is a chunk smaller than that of the candle to permit for a snugger in shape. Considering that is a candleholder, do no longer hollow the smooth too deeply.

At this component, you can pick out to feature a personal touch to the candleholder thru using growing a grove to function inlay materials like a pop of coloration.

To make certain that the cloth remains in location, upload a thin layer of glue along the grove and try to make it neat.

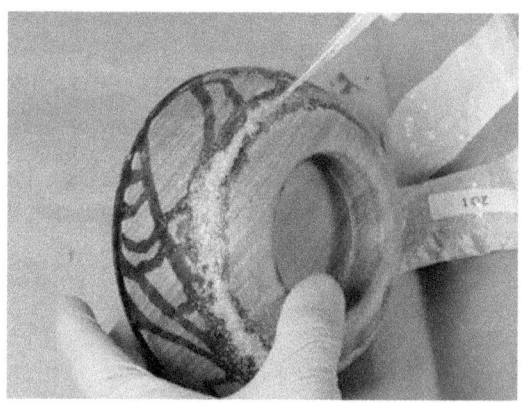

Finish it with the aid of sanding every the outdoors and interior additives the usage of sandpaper.

To art work on the bottom a part of the candleholder, unmount the candleholder and join a smaller jaw chew as a way to increase in the hollow created for a less attackable maintain.

Next, you will use a bowl gouge to smoothen out the lowest of the holder.

After you're happy with the form made, sand it down till you get a smoother end.

Finish it up through manner of utilizing a coat of oil to deal with the wooden and make it long

lasting for longer.

Leave it to dry, and then you could start the usage of your candleholder.

Honey Dipper

Materials Needed

Roughing gouge

Spindle gouge

Sandpaper

Parting tool

Food secure mineral oil for completing

60-diploma live center

Art makers

Woodblock of two" x2" x8"

Band observed

Spur pressure

Pencil

Ruler

Wire burners

How to Make a Honey Dipper

Start via making geared up the piece of wood.

On one forestall of the wooden clean, create grooves the use of the bandsaw so that you can help to connect it to the lathe through the spur pressure. This helps to save you the wooden from cracking up from the pressure.

On the opposite quit of the blank, trace its middle with the resource of drawing diagonal lines. This is in which the 60-diploma live center will press via the smooth.

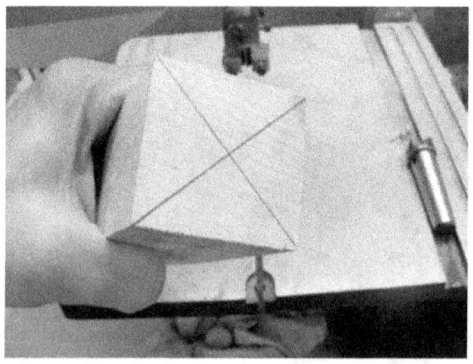

Mount the plank of wooden onto the lathe. The clean may be have come to be the numerous stay center and the spur strain. While walking, attempt to maintain about a ¼ inch distance amongst your smooth and the tool rest.

Once the block is because it need to be positioned, flip the motor on and start turning the wooden.

To advantage a cylindrical form, use a roughing gauge and a spindle gouge interchangeably. You ought to preserve repositioning the device rest as you switch the wooden.

To create the honey dipping aspect, use a parting tool to create the grooves. You need to try to equal the space most of the grooves, like about ¼ of an inch.

Using a spindle gouge, upload multiple beads at the deal with detail. In among the beads, cord-burn it to add more data via including a black line in amongst. To wire-burn, maintain the wires on every side even as placing them in most of the areas created thru the beads. Turn the lathe on, and as it turns, it's going to create friction, resulting in some smoke leaving in the again of a darkish line.

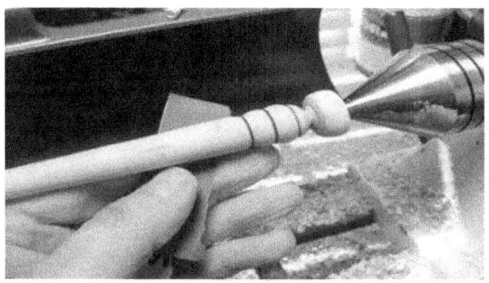

Finish the piece by means of the usage of manner of sanding it right down to get a smoother finish.

With the lathe off, mark the beads the use of the markers, or you can even pick out to dye it a coloration of your preference; you may go together with black and yellow to mimic a bee's shade.

Remember to cut off the ends at the manipulate and the dipping element, then sand

it off.

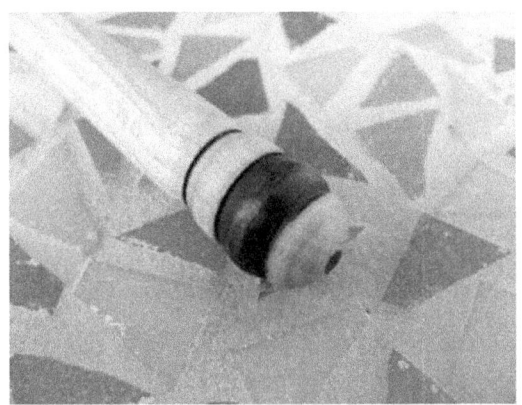

After it dries out, follow a coat of oil to cope with the timber. You can now begin dipping it in honey.

Rolling Pin

Materials Needed

Roughing gouge

Skew chisel

Hardwood easy of timber thirteen' lengthy

Oil

Sandpaper

Live middle

Drive center

Pencil

Ruler

Wire burners

How to Make a Rolling Pin

Start thru marking out the middle of the wooden. You can try this through drawing diagonal strains at some stage in the timber's corners, then marking out the intersection.

Mount the wooden at the lathe with the pressure middle at the headstock and the stay middle in the tail inventory.

Using the roughing gouge to eliminate materials from the timber to smoothen it out.

Keep at this until the timber smooth turns into cylindrical all through.

At this issue, you could use the skew chisel to even it out.

To paintings at the rolling pin, you need to degree same lengths from the cease to a point on the pin on each elements to cowl the tapered ends.

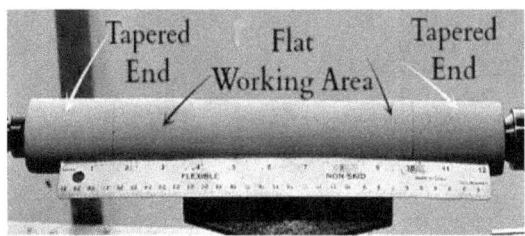

Mark out the regions with a pencil to behave as a manual while turning the piece.

To form the tapered ends, you will attitude the tool rest and, the use of the skew chisel, form out the ends of the pin as a lot as the marked component.

As you determine on the ends, maintain smoothening out the center element, and while completed, run your fingers alongside it to verify whether or now not there are any imperfections.

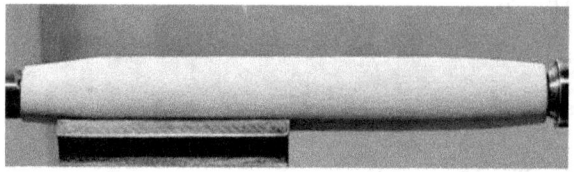

After you have got were given smoothened out the pin, use sandpaper to characteristic the completing touches to it.

You can select out to move away your pin like this or determine to feature some decorations to it.

So next, take the skew chisel and mark out grooves on points along the handles. Using the burning wires, burn a darkish line on the wooden.

When finished, sand it down and alongside every grit, use a chunk of material to wipe it down. To do away with the rolling pin from the lathe, use a parting tool to take away the more wooden at the ends, then sand it down as you pass.

To stop off, exercise a layer of food-stable oil and go away it to dry.

You can now use your pin to roll out your dough.

Wooden Spatula

Material wanted

Food stable mineral oil

Burning wires

Sandpaper

Spindle gouge

Skew chisel

Spur strength

Live middle

Measuring tape

Marker

Wood clean 11 inches lengthy

Bandsaw

Hacksaw

Roughing gouge

How to Make a Wooden Spatula

Start with the resource of marking out the popular dimensions on the piece of wooden.

Next, trim off the timber using the bandsaw, leaving the difficulty in which the address is supposed to be thicker than the relaxation of the timber.

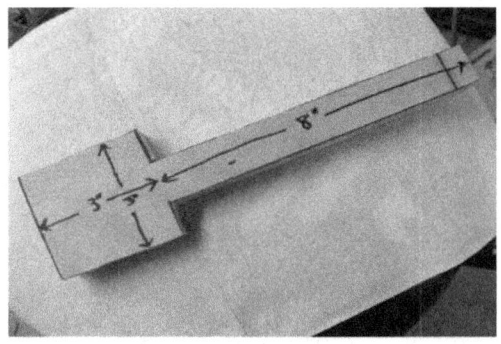

Using the bandsaw, create grooves for use to connect the spur strain thru the wooden. This lets in prevent the wood from splitting due to the pressure done.

On the opportunity surrender, the use of a pencil and a ruler, draw the diagonals from one corner to the opportunity. Mark out the intersection and press the live middle into the wood through it.

Next, connect the spur stress to the headstock and the stay middle to the headstock with the timber clean in the middle.

Turn the lathe on and ensure that the wooden blank is nicely-balanced and turns easily.

Start off via rounding off the spatula aspect the usage of a roughing gouge and a spindle gouge. At this level, do not virtually smoothen out the spatula cease because of the reality this can be used to shape out its very last shape.

As you drift, paintings at the contend with element truely barely earlier than the deal with in which the bulge of the spatula starts offevolved. To do that, you could want to reposition the tool relaxation and mindset the roughing gouge to get a more precise reduce as you switch the plank of wood. Use the shearing technique for these cuts.

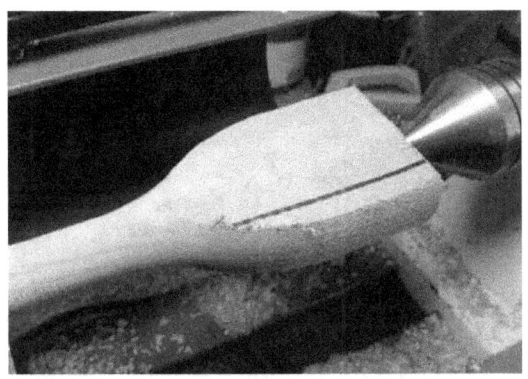

Next, begin turning the deal with element. Round it off as you pass. Using a parting device, add grooves at the deal with, which you may later use a burning twine to function a darkish line for adornment on.

Smoothen it out, and using a hacksaw, reduce it off the lathe and smoothen the give up of the deal with too. Ensure that it's miles grew to become off for protection earlier than you narrow the spatula from the lathe.

Using a sharpie or a stencil of the spatula, mark out the shapes of the perimeters of the spatula.

Using the bandsaw, reduce outside the traces and sand it down certainly. For this step, it's miles nice to use a belt sander. However, make certain that you do no longer make it too thin on the equal time as sanding.

When glad with the form finished, apply a layer of the oil on the spatula, wipe it off using a paper towel, and then you may use it.

Pepper Mill and Matching Salt Shaker

Materials Needed

Two timber blanks

Four jaw scroll chuck

Finishing oil

stay middle

Forstner bits

Grinding mechanism for the pepper mill

Epoxy

Robust cone center

How to Make a Pepper Mill and Matching Salt Shaker

To make certain that the inside and outside of your gadgets are concentric with every precise, you need to begin with the inside detail and then paintings on the outdoor.

This additionally makes it much less complex for the four jaws chuck to grip as you drill.

With the 4 jaw gripping on one detail of the clean, connect it to the headstock, then use a

60-diploma live center to region the other stop at the tail stock.

Using the Forstner drill, create a recess in the piece of wooden about 1 ½ of the entire block period deep.

While running in this, ensure that the bore is huge enough to house the grinding mechanism.

Do this via using lateral stress collectively together with your scrapper and maintaining proper alignment with the stop of the billet.

As you switch the easy, you need to preserve attempting out whether or not the factors healthful properly to keep away from overdoing it. Later, you can use epoxy to attach the additives in location while completed.

To now art work at the outer detail, seize the recess with a Robust cone middle on the identical time as the other factor is positioned in location the usage of the spigot jaws.

Turn the outdoor using the mortise chisel through the shearing approach to preserve it to form.

For the salt shaker, use the equal 4-jaw chuck to preserve in place after which drill into it to approximately ¼ of its period.

Next, you'll need to form the pinnacle in which the top of the shaker may be located after which smoothen it out.

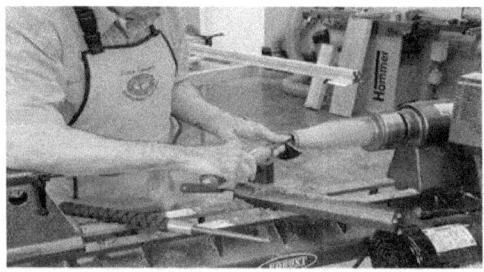

Repeat the earlier method to expose the outer a part of the shaker using the chisel.

Finish up by manner of putting the tops on each the shaker and pepper mill.

Sand the wooden down after which exercise a layer of oil to guard the timber.

Wooden Egg

Materials Needed

Spindle gouge

Bowling gouge

Sandpaper

Woods for the assignment (2" x3")

Artisan dye

Finishing supply

Marker

Ruler

Pencil

Chuck

Skew chisel

How to Make an Egg From Wood

If you must upload a pop of colour to the egg, use lighter-colored wood to make the colour pop out extra.

On each forestall of the block, mark out the center thru drawing diagonals from each nook and marking the intersection because of the reality the middle.

Mount the wooden on the lathe thru the middle.

Start rounding off the piece of timber the use of a bowling gouge.

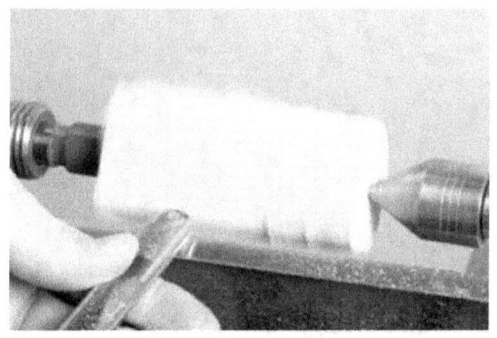

Now, reduce a tenon on one forestall of the clean in which the 4 jaw chuck can be placed. For this, you may want to apply a skew chisel.

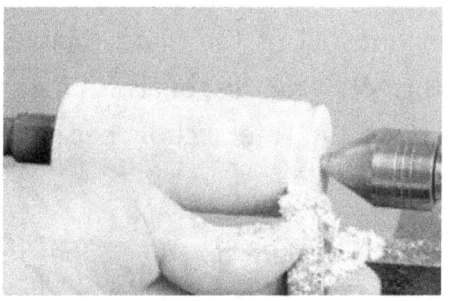

With the lathe off, attach the chuck to the wood through the tenon you honestly made.

Start turning the egg using a spindle gouge to get a greater particular form. You can constantly pick out an egg to behave as a manual as you switch the wooden blank.

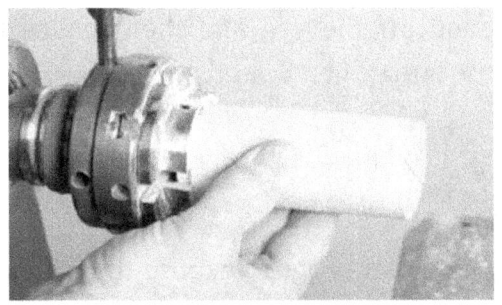

Once you are happy with the shape executed, sand the egg down the use of sandpaper.

You can pick out to feature the dye to the egg, and for this, it is probably higher to use a sanding sealer to make certain the even distribution of the shade dye at the egg.

With the lathe strolling low, use a material to evenly comply with the dye to the egg until the appropriate consistency is accomplished. Because the factor of touch some of the egg and the lathe is small, make certain to keep the egg in area to save you it from falling off.

Next, you can need to apply the extended thing of the skew chisel to part of the egg such that the dye does now not run off everywhere in the egg. Ensure that the lathe remains on a gradual run to avoid digging deep into the egg.

Now sand off the egg and then reduce it off from the lathe, then sand the quit down too.

Apply a layer of finish to the egg, and you're executed.

You can do extra eggs to expose them in a bowl or a crate.

Bottle Stopper

Materials Needed

Bottle stopper

Wood clean

Chuck and jaws

Thick glue

Sandpaper

Drill bits

Skew chisel

Roughing gouge

Spindle gouge

Drill chuck

Revolving middle

Varnish finishes

Paste wax

Mandreal stud

Steel wool

How to Make a Bottle Stopper

Mark the clean's middle on every factors by using manner of drawing diagonals from one corner to the alternative, then marking the intersection.

Mount the woodchuck at the lathe, mount the piece of wooden, after which flip the lathe on at

a speed of ,500 rpm.

It is probably first-rate in case you used a skew

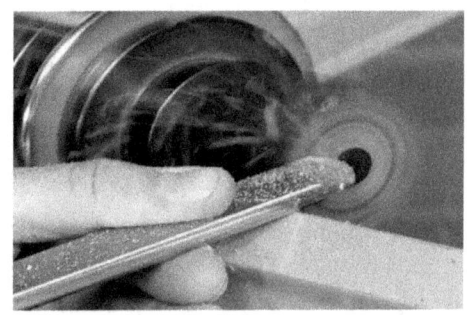

chisel to real out the give up of the

smooth and, at the same time as at it, create a dip to help center the drill.

The drill bit is based totally upon at the shape of wood you have got had been given. A softer timber requires a smaller-sized bit as compared to hardwood.

After measuring the mandrel stud, add ¼ to at the least one/8 of an inch to ensure which you hire the whole thread — mark this factor with tape to manual you as you switch the relaxation of the timber.

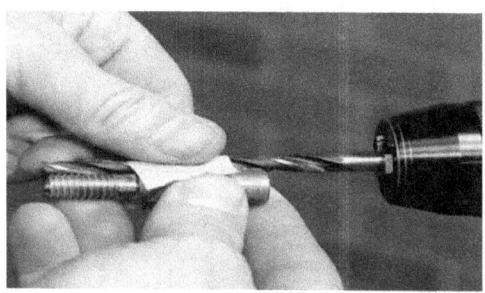

With the bit and drill chuck at the tail stock, flip the lathe on at a slower price of approximately 700 rpm to prevent warmth from constructing up.

As you switch, hold advancing the drill until you get to the factor wherein you had taped it.

With the woodchuck even though connected, tap the blank. For this, you could pick out to use a wrench or a faucet address with the useful resource of advancing in a unmarried turn and then retreating in 1 / 4 turn, which relieves the chips. Keep doing this until the faucet in the end bottoms out.

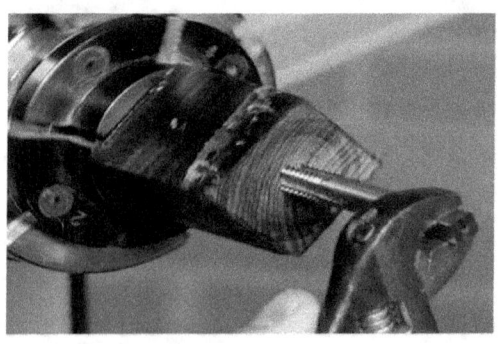

With the smooth tapped at this element, mount the bottle stopper and thread it at the easy, preserving off over-tightening it considering how sensitive the threads are.

Start the lathe all over again at a velocity of ,500 rpm and begin turning the clean the usage of a roughing gouge. Be cautious to make smaller cuts even as dealing with the tool at this tempo to keep away from getting a capture, which may spoil your form.

Turn the bottle stopper for your most famous form at the same time as preserving close to the pushing to get the excellent healthful.

Now, with the tail inventory off, you could flip the pinnacle of the stopper slightly with small cuts until the right shape is accomplished.

Using a six hundred grit, sand the bottle stopper on the lathe, retaining it at a gradual tempo of about seven hundred rpm to avoid warmth construct-up.

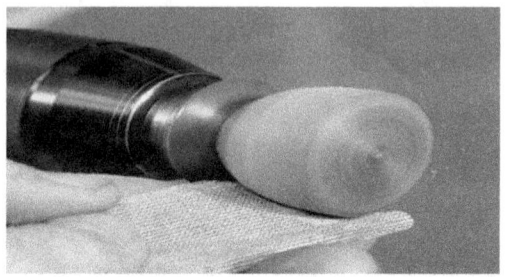

After you've got smoothened it out, exercise a quit to defend the wooden. Do this in layers and depart it for approximately 24 hours to in reality remedy.

With the lathe however on, practice a layer of wax on steel wool and run it on the bottle stopper for a smoother finish.

Remove the stopper from the lathe, and for a greater stable finish, upload glue even as threading the bottle stopper collectively. You can do this via utilising glue to the drilled hole after which threading the stud in.

Leave the glue to dry and upload the droplet to finish the project.

Mason Jar Lid

Materials Needed

Turning clean of approximately 2" x 4"

Sandpaper

Food strong oil

Roughing gouge

Mason jar

Live center

spur middle

band saw

measuring tape

Multi jawed chuck

Bowl gouge

Spindle gouge

Parting tool

How to Make a Mason Jar Lid

Start with the aid of measuring the mouth of your mason jar, then switch the duration to the piece of timber, accounting for the cloth you could lose whilst turning the wood.

Next, mount the blank many of the facilities and start rounding it off using the roughing gouge.

On one give up of the smooth, create a tenon to mount the jawed chuck to help even as turning.

After growing the tenon, turn the lathe off, mount the jawed chuck onto the pinnacle inventory, and insert the blank. Center the clean in region by way of manner of the use of repositioning the tail stock while tightening the maintain.

Using the bowling gouge, start smoothening the cease of the smooth. How big your cuts get can be depending on how a long manner the blank is from the woodchuck. This guarantees that the clean stays focused at the same time as you switch it.

Once the face meets your expectancies, reduce a tenon as a manual, and use your jar to try and in shape it in vicinity.

After making sure that the jar suits thru the tenon, turn it to about ½" to make sure that it suits snugly within the jar. At this trouble, you can decide how massive you would love the lid to be. Use this length to decide how a tremendous deal further you can need to expose it.

When carried out, stop it up with the resource of the usage of sanding it down and the usage of the food-regular oil to supply it.

Now you could want to use a slim parting tool to split the lid from the easy.

After you've got were given got controlled to reduce it off, put off the clean from the woodchuck and replace it with the lid, with the interior detail performing as the tenon. To avoid leaving marks behind from being held through the chuck, layer some paper towels across the tenon, then insert it into the woodchuck.

Turn the outside part of the lid on your pride. Finish through sanding it down, then take away it from the lathe.

If your lid does no longer wholesome as snugly as you may have was hoping, you can generally tie an elastic band around the jar to make it more solid.

Wood Turned Lamp

Materials Needed

Wood blanks of various sizes

Roughing gouge

Sandpaper

Drill bits

Wiring cable

Lamp harp

Bulb kit

How To Make A Wooden Lamp

Start through mounting the wooden clean on the lathe the various centers.

This need to be executed after you have got had been given recognized the middle of the timber lank by using manner of drawing diagonals and marking out the intersection.

Using a roughing gouge, turn the wooden right into a round form.

Since this venture requires stacking of the rounded blanks to make a stand, you will be required to mount the opportunity blanks and spherical them off too.

Use the sanding device to smoothen the blanks till they're properly rounded off.

Treat the timber through making use of a completing oil.

Keep repeating this till you're happy with the peak attained after stacking them up.

Next, you could want to drill holes within the rounded woods the use of a drill bit. Starting with the lowest clean, drill a hollow at the center and upload some distinctive one on the side at the way for use later to bypass the electric cable thru.

To get a extra exciting shape, drill holes at particular points on the opposite blocks.

When performed making the holes, use the wiring cable to connect them together via manner of passing it through the holes you had drilled earlier.

With some number one wiring abilities, you could join the bulb bundle to the lamp harp and then be part of it to the socket.

Wooden Bangles

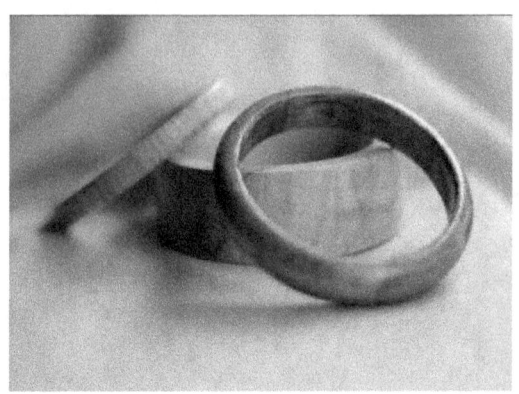

Materials Needed

Chuck jaw

Roughing gouge

Wood clean

Tape diploma

Band noticed

Parting tool

Drill bits

How to Make a Wooden Bangle

You can start via measuring out the width of your wrist or friend's wrist to manual you on how huge the bangle is probably.

Next, you could want to switch this length onto the piece of wood and mark it out.

Using your observed, reduce out the extra a part of the wooden leaving inside the again of a ½ of an inch to account for the material so one may be eliminated at the same time as turning the piece of wooden. Since we do not intend to use the complete wooden, you may lessen it right into a smaller length, relying on the intensity of your woodchuck.

Find a hard center of the block and drill a hole huge enough to match a bug screw for the woodchuck.

After you have got installation it on the lathe using the chuck, begin rounding it and flattening it the use of a roughing gouge.

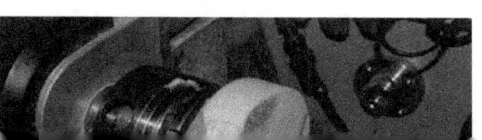

Using a sharpened parting tool, element the internal diameter of the chunk.

Keep the use of the tool at the same time as making remedy cuts; keep in mind to stop at the equal time as you're approximately ¾ deep into the wood's depth.

Next, unscrew the block from the chuck and then flit it such that the middle piece created acts as a tenon that is gripped through the usage of way of the chuck.

Repeat the equal method on this extraordinary thing. The motive right right here is to eliminate the inner a part of the bangle.

Once the interior issue falls off, start sanding the inner a part of the bangle, being cautious not to harm yourself at the woodchuck jaws.

After sanding it down, smoothen the outer element with the lathe walking at a slower pace to avoid getting a capture that might damage the thread of the bangle.

Next, use the pointy parting tool to lessen the bangle from the block.

Be cautious as you chop not to hit the jaws of the chuck. Ensure that you first mark out the width of the bangle so you could have a guide as you narrow.

Once the bangle falls off from the block, sand it down, then wax it.

Wood Lidded Box

Materials Needed

Four jaw chuck

spindle gouge

Parting device

spindle gouge

Wood easy

Pencil

Ruler

Live center

Scraper

Calipers

Drill bit

How to Make a Wood Lidded Box

Start with the useful resource of getting geared up the wood clean with the aid of the usage of drawing out diagonals on every detail of the wooden from one nook to the possibility. The intersection will act because the middle.

Mount the timber onto the lathe a number of the centers.

Turn the lathe on and tough out the block the usage of a roughing gouge to supply it to a spherical form.

Using a parting tool, shape a tenon on each side of the block to offer higher gripping for the 4 jaw chuck.

One of the tenon is probably used to grip the lid, at the identical time as the opposite acts as a base.

Turn the lathe off and do away with the force center from the lathe and replace it with the jaw chuck. Reposition the tail inventory for higher assist.

Using a pointy parting tool, separate the top detail from the lowest with the aid of manner of developing a slender kerf.

As the bottom is ready to interrupt up from the block, gradual the lathe down and maintain the lowest, stopping it from falling and getting broken.

Turn off the lathe and separate the bottom from the relaxation of the block.

Using a spindle gouge, flip the lid's internal at approximately 1/8th of an inch from the outdoor part of the tenon.

Using a scraping tool, make a dome shape at the middle part of the lid.

Make your cuts from the inner, transferring within the route of the outside. When glad with

the final consequences, sand it all the way all of
the way all the way down to smoothen it out.

Using calipers, diploma the diameter of the lid.

Next, cast off the lid from the chuck and mount
the alternative part of the block.

Reduce the diameter to about 1/8th of an inch
and switch it to the base. By reducing the
diameter, you create greater wiggle room for
the reduce to be made on the outlet of the
base.

To well mark out the diameter of the lowest,
flip the lathe on at low tempo and region the
caliper's jaws on the lowest such that because
the lathe turns, the calipers rating the bottom.

You will then use a spindle gouge to reveal the top of the bottom.

Now, use a scrapper to hollow out the pinnacle of the bottom sizeable enough to cover the scribes created thru the calipers.

Start widening the mortise the usage of a parting tool. The tenon at the lid must snugly in shape in the mortise of the bottom.

Have the lathe taking walks sluggish as you're making thin cuts to avoid overcutting, in case you need to have an impact on the in form.

As you get inside the direction of attaining a cushty in shape, use a pencil to trace across the tenon. As you hold becoming it in area, the markings will switch to the mortise, acting as a manual.

Ensure that the lid does now not in shape so tightly for the motive that this might destroy the piece as you try to dispose of it.

After the lid has been prepared, start shaping the whole field the use of a spindle gouge and with the tail inventory in region.

Next, get rid of the tail inventory and turn the lid once more to smoothen it out. Ensure that the bevel stays in touch with the lid to keep away from getting a trap at the same time as making small cuts.

When executed, sand it down.

Remove the lid from the lowest and, the usage of the calipers, degree the diameter of the sector at its narrowest aspect. This will decide the size of the drill for use. You may even want to subtract about 1/four" from the diameter.

On the tail inventory, mount a Forstner bit to bore a hole at the field. As you drift, hold eliminating the shavings from the box in order now not to over drill. Ensure which you leave about ¼" thickness to permit room for sanding the lowest.

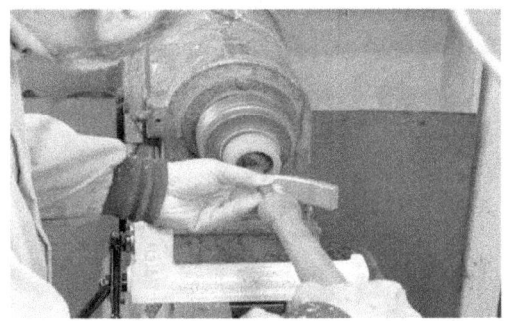

Smoothen the indoors of the world with a bowl scraper. Make very small cuts so as no longer to damage the shape already created.

When carried out, sand the whole piece down collectively with the lid and then comply with a layer of oil to treat the wood.

Use a parting tool to split the bottom from the chuck, after which sand it down too.

Your area is prepared for gifting.

Chair Leg Spindle

Materials Needed

Roughing gouge

Wood clean

Live center

Skew chisel

Calipers

Parting device

Pencil

Sandpaper

Spindle gouge

Ruler

How to Make a Chair Leg Spindle

Start through sporting your protecting system.

Next, determine the center of the wooden by using drawing the diagonals and locating the intersection.

Mount the clean onto the lathe and bring the tail stock up.

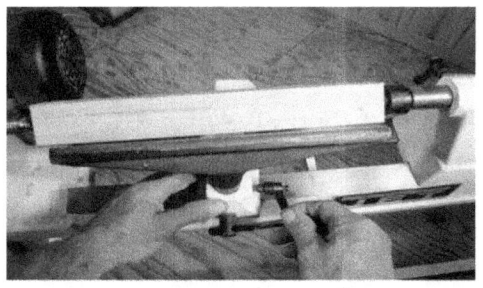

Start the lathe, and the use of a roughing gouge, flip the smooth till it's miles rounded off with the resource of way of getting rid of all the corners.

Ensure that the lathe is at a low velocity to provide you enough manipulate as you turn.

For this step, you may want to make push cuts and make sure the device rest is near enough to the wooden clean without touching it.

Next, you'll use a skew chisel to smoothen the clean and make sure it gets a cylindrical shape throughout and not the usage of a difficult edges. You can boost up the lathe at this thing.

Depending on how you need your spindle to look, you may decide to characteristic beads or coves to it.

With your spindle now smoothened out, take the pencil and mark in which you would really like the coves or beads to be created.

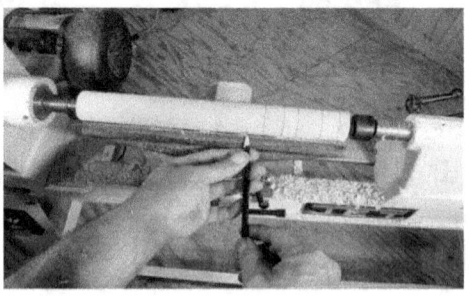

To get the coves, you'll need to use a spindle gouge and work your way from the pinnacle to the lowest. Using a slender spindle gouge creates higher coves thinking about you can get deeper and slender cuts.

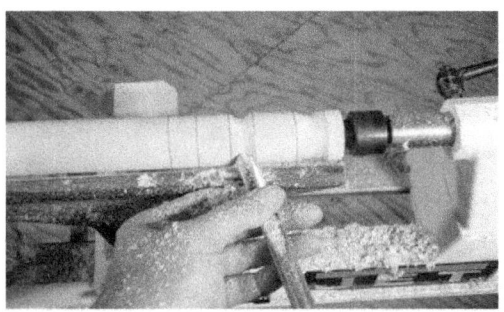

For the beads, you may need to use a skew chisel. You will want to hold the skew flat at the device rest, aligning it with the marks you made with the pencil.

To make the cuts, make certain that the decreasing tip of the skew is positioned right at the pencil marks whilst the relaxation of the decreasing place is balanced on the bead region.

Repeat this on the opportunity facet of the bead till the shape supposed is executed.

To art work at the diameters, select out the calipers and switch your selected diameter to the spindle. Make cuts the use of a parting device, growing grooves. As you narrow, keep checking out the diameter with the calipers to live in line.

Remove the waste on the groove the use of a skew until you're glad with the brand new diameters.

Remember to maintain shifting the device rest in the direction of the spindle without touching it as you figure.

Next, use the sanding paper to smoothen it out after which lessen it off from the lathe and smoothen the ends too.

Apply a layer of finishing oil, and you're well to transport. Repeat this on the other spindles to get the 4 spindles to in shape to your chair.

Christmas Tree

Materials Needed

Parting tool

Skew chisel

Spindle gouge

Live center

Brass pin

Steb-kind pressure middle

Woodchuck

Morse taper drill chuck

Sandpaper

2 blocks of severa sizes

Band observed

Wood polish

Glue

Calipers

Jacobs chuck

Drive center

How to Make a Christmas Tree

Start by using mounting the wood piece on the lathe in among the centers.

Using a skew, difficult the block off to a round form.

After rounding it off, use the skew to create a tenon if you want to be used with the chuck at the lathe.

To get a better suit, use the calipers to switch the diameter of the chuck at the smooth to make a tenon so as to snugly in shape in the various jaws of the chuck.

When carried out, you can want to mount the block inside the woodchuck and tighten it in vicinity after mounting the chuck on the lathe.

The thing set up on the chuck will function the tree's base, at the equal time as the opposite detail that is furthest from the chuck will artwork due to the fact the pinnacle part of the tree wherein the ornament can be positioned.

Use the skew to flatten out the top a part of the tree and ensure that it is rectangular to the duration.

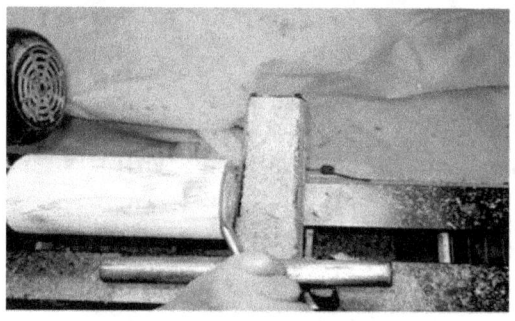

Mount a Jacobs chuck on the lathe's tail stock and drill a hollow at the top of the clean, that permits you for use to position the decoration. Use a drill of approximately 1/8th of an inch and drill it to approximately half "deep into the block on the center.

At this factor, the tree's frame is finished, and now you may need to eliminate it from the lathe and mount the smaller block for the decoration.

Since the small block could possibly effortlessly shatter whilst drilled on, upload a Steb-kind pressure center in vicinity of the woodchuck. This particular one is better than a normal pressure center as it does not require pre-drilling.

On one problem of the smooth, create a tenon so that you can be used to mount a woodchuck that has smaller jaws.

Once installation, difficult it to a spherical shape too.

As performed in advance on the bigger blank, drill the hollow on the middle.

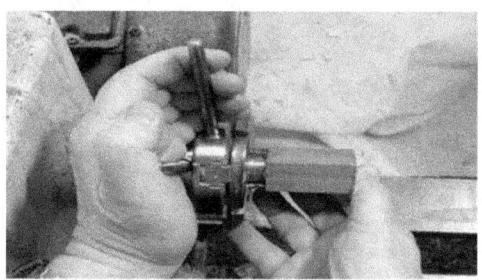

Next, unmount the smaller lock after which insert a brass pin inside the hollow created and join it to the bigger clean via the hole too. Add glue to ensure it's far absolutely regular.

With the 2 portions joined together, use the roughing gouge to spherical it off.

Using a skew, begin developing the conical shape of the Christmas tree on the bigger block.

Make peeling cuts to take away most of the cloth.

Proceed downwards to ensure you acquire the form at a few stage inside the wooden piece.

Remember that the tree's base wants to e thicker than the pinnacle of it. You can mark out the lowest of the tree at this aspect using the skew.

Determining the lowest of the tree will manual you higher on the same time as turning the easy.

Next, waft to the decoration piece and flip it proper into a conical shape too.

At the lowest of the ornament, make a ball form the usage of a small skew.

After growing the ball, begin developing beads, making small cuts in order not to area lots of stress at the clean.

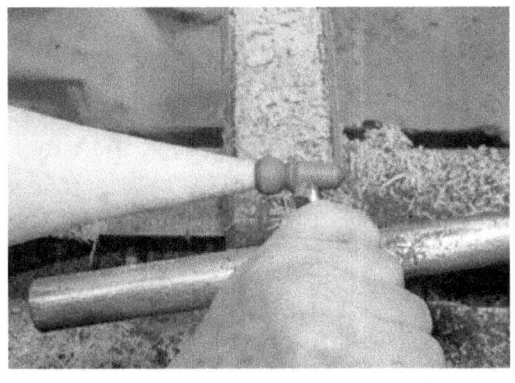

For protection measures, add a small decoration on the top of the decoration simply so the top isn't as sharp.

Move to the tree's body by way of using first smoothening the pinnacle wherein the decoration and the tree meet.

An inch from the base of the tree, begin marking intervals of about an inch if you want to behave because the boughs of the tree.

Use a skew to create those capabilities on the tree, making very small cuts.

Turn a concave slope from the lowest place to the pinnacle part on every layer.

Using an in depth gouge, preserve defining the concave slope until the tree boughs start taking form.

As for the bottom, make a concave slope too. For a better look, make sure that its diameter is half of of the lowest bough layer.

At this aspect, the tree is finished. So take the sandpaper and start sanding the tree down, starting from one hundred and fifty grits to 1000 grit.

Next, follow a friction polish to complete up with the tree.

You can exercise a layer of wax to the tree to present it a shinier cease.

Using a parting tool, remove the tree from the lathe.

Weed Pots

Materials Needed

Bowl gouge

Roughing gouge

Parting tool

Wood clean

band noticed

Woodchuck

Round nostril scraper

Jacobs chuck

How to Make a Weed Pot

Start with the aid of the use of prepping your piece of timber, then mount it at the lathe. You can start with the aid of the usage of trimming off the rims the usage of a band observed to get a extra specific form to make the turning gadget easier.

Mount the wood maximum of the facilities, then begin turning the smooth proper into a spherical form the use of a roughing gouge.

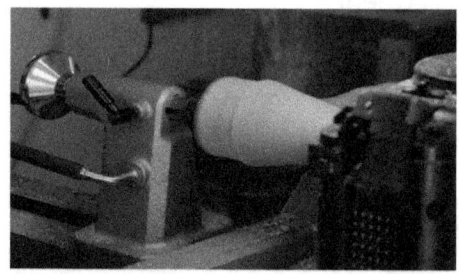

Next, create a tenon on one element of the blank, so that you can be used to mount the woodchuck.

Move the tail inventory in the direction of the clean for additonal resource after converting the spur electricity with the woodchuck.

Start roughing out the clean the use of a bowling gouge with the lathe on. You will need to emerge as privy to which end acts due to the fact the bottom as you go with the flow to make the very last shape.

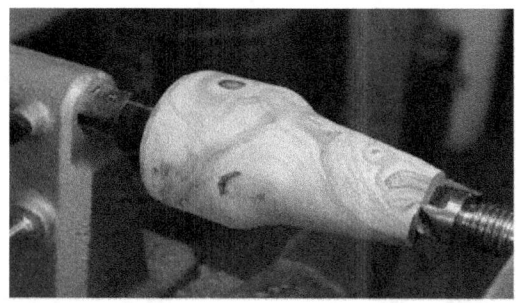

After carrying out a close to sufficient shape, get rid of the tail stock, glide the device rest toward the top of the pot, then smoothen it.

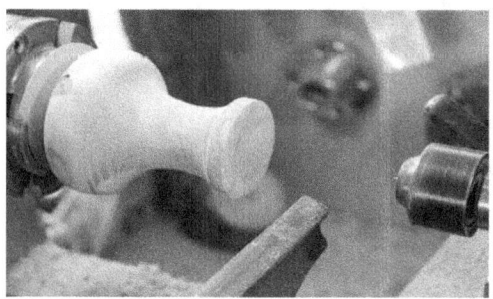

Next, you want to drill a hole within the pot to create room for putting the flora.

Mount the Jacobs chuck onto the lathe with a drill of an out ¼", then study it up with a bigger drill bit.

Ensure that the hole is deep sufficient for the stems of the vegetation to take a seat without falling off.

When finished, use your spherical nose scraper to shape the pinnacle of the vase near the holes created.

Start sanding it all the way all the way all the way down to accurate any imperfections created whilst turning.

Afterward, coat the vase with a layer of oil or finishing polish.

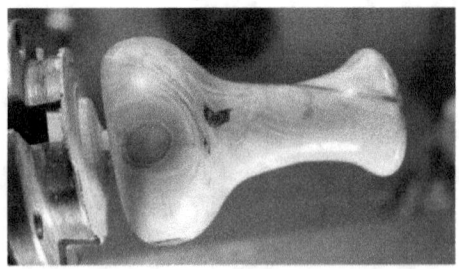

150

After you're finished, use a parting device to eliminate the pot from the lathe, then sand off the lowest element too.

Chapter 6: Safety and Maintenance

Safety and maintenance are vital whilst you are busy with a woodworking challenge. After all, working with less than 5 arms can be a bit hard except you're up for a venture! But no, we want to make sure we're blanketed from any viable harm or incidents.

There are a few protection precautions to take in advance than and throughout your mission. Safety measures, protection gadget, ventilation, dust collection, and device safety are important to test. Shop safety is also very vital, but we will now pass into detail on the manner to prepare yourself to create artwork!

Taking Safety Measures

A short inspection is vital to make certain your workshop and tools are clean and secure to begin operating. Conditions of woodworkers' workshops can range considerably, from pristine offices to the ones wherein system is buried beneath dust and off-cuts. In popular, tidiness is a tremendous indicator of methods efficaciously one-of-a-type safety issues are addressed with the resource of that woodworker; but, in case you're a messy timber employee like me and every now and then neglect about it, you are not on my own!

All system need to be properly-maintained and feature good enough protection measures in location, together with slicing guards. Make certain you've got got been nicely taught and licensed to apply any tool on your workshop. A mistake in a woodshop may additionally want to price you a finger.

There must be effective controls in place to reduce the fitness dangers posed through wood dirt. Dust may be a pain, particularly in case you're allergic and you sneeze at some point of an vital decreasing element and decrease off greater than you need to, growing a totally unstable stool. It can motive dermatitis or bronchial allergic reactions because of physically coping with or breathing in unstable chemical materials that a few dust incorporates.

Make sure to test via instructions that cover the following subjects:

- tool schooling and supervision

- fitness chance facts

- the way to position on and contend with dirt mask

- a manner to nicely smooth up

- consistent clothing at the same time as running

These are things to offer a brief inspection in advance than you flow into at once to more specific protection and safety factors.

Safety Equipment and Tool Maintenance

When operating with wood, there are various specific styles of volatile gear. So until you want a loose nail lessen, permit's ensure to use protection gadget! Make it a addiction to apply protection system from the beginning, and you can by no means want to art work with out it. Be positive to maintain and take pleasure for your machine, too!

Safety Glasses

Are you scared of getting dust and debris for your eyes? Safety glasses can help shield your eyes, which embody your face, from any volatile pieces of timber and dirt. Most safety glasses are created with stable lenses that could produce tons less effect if debris hits your eyes. It is likewise recommended to get safety glasses with component presentations that guard your face from large and sharper pieces of waste, which may be very unstable thinking about strength equipment can fling particles at an top notch velocity.

Face Guards

When working with extra large portions of wood that require extra elbow grease, many big debris becomes airborne or slip, probable resulting in a risky scenario. If you are the usage of protection glasses with out facet guards, I suggest wearing a face protect, or protect, over your safety glasses. Face shields can soak up a number of the effect of flying particles and allows to keep flying debris from moving into your face and eyes. I as quickly as look at of a person whose nose ended up damaged from a large piece of debris even as he end up timber turning; however, had he now not had that protect on, the airborne materials might also want to have achieved to his face what they did to the face defend. It became overwhelmed, dented, and so forth. Believe it or no longer, although, it changed into no longer cracked or

damaged.

Face Masks and Respirators

Getting dust and smaller particles into your lungs and frame is a fitness hazard, even worse if it's miles risky chemical substances. Inhaling dirt and chemical substances is inevitable at the same time as you do woodworking. For your protection, it's far advocated which you use a face mask to save you dust from being inhaled and respirators to reduce the danger of any chemical fumes you would possibly inhale.

Hearing Protection

Jumping at least ten toes excessive from a stunning loud noise isn't amusing, however hearing safety will save you that for you. Did you apprehend that sure woodworking system, which encompass planers or routers, can put off excessive decibels that are dangerous on your ears and can damage your being attentive to? All you need is a tough and speedy of excellent fitted earmuffs and earplugs! They provide safety on your ears and prevent any dirt and smaller debris from getting into your ear.

Clothes

Clothes? Why might garments need to be a precaution? It's honestly cloth, right?

Clothing might not appear to be a huge deal to us, however it is able to become one of the maximum volatile subjects while doing woodwork. For example, if you have free clothing on, it may be stuck thru the blade at the identical time as you are decreasing, as an instance, and turn out to be entangled; this will bring about your hand being jerked beforehand and arms is probably detached or maimed. Loose-becoming gloves can do the equal element, which took place to someone I understand just currently. His hand have emerge as jerked so rapid and with such force that he lost fingertips and tore the ligaments in his thumb. This isn't alleged to scare you, however topics which include this arise every day and you need to be aware about your clothing, carrying appropriate clothing (typically lengthy sleeves and pants). Strong metallic-toed shoes can save you topics from falling onto your feet.

Jewelry

It's comprehensible absolutely everyone has a favorite piece of jewelry they like to position on, however did it get up to you that this sentimental object must turn out to be a safety chance in the workshop? Necklaces are very risky; like unfastened apparel, they're able to get stuck within the blade and injure you from the sudden jerk or pull you in the path of the brink. A ring can without problem get caught on a chunk of device, as nicely, at the aspect of bracelets and watches. If you do have any rings on you, it's miles high-quality to both not put on them the least bit or to region them in a stable place.

Disconnecting Power Tools

If it's switched off, it is solid, right? Wrong—energy tool however have power internal them despite the truth that have become off. If you haven't in reality disconnected the tool from its strength deliver (i.E., the hole it have become plugged into), then you may be busy converting a few factor at the electricity tool, and there's a opportunity of it being by way of chance switched on and injuring you.

Alcohol and Medication

I understand you've heard which you need to by no means pressure below the have an impact on of alcohol or tablets; and doesn't it appear to be maximum drug treatments have warnings on the bottles about now not walking heavy equipment until you understand how that specific remedy will have an effect on you? The cause is that impairment from any of these gadgets alters your notion and reflexes, further to your popularity and hobby. Since you'll probable be walking with probably unstable gadget, it's far now not encouraged to be below the have an impact on of alcohol or medicinal capsules that could flip a chilled night time time of woodcrafting proper into a trip to the emergency room.

Sharp Blades vs. Dull Blades

One would probably count on that silly blades are secure and sharp blades risky, but it's in truth the other! Dull blades gradual you down, damage your substances (silly blades can get hot and burn the timber), and makes you work extra difficult to pressure the device, which can emerge as causing an harm if the device jerks or actions closer to you. A sharp blade can offer you with easy cuts, fewer splinters, and won't have a outstanding force if it occurs to jam. Always make certain all your blades are sharp!

Old Nails Inside Wood

Many of us like to create some thing definitely one-of-a-kind from vintage timber, but every so often nails may be embedded so deep interior, the nails can't be discovered until it's far too past due. To prevent any nails from being flung towards you, a metallic detector may be your pleasant buddy in this. A metallic detector will stumble upon the nails within the timber that aren't visible. This steel detector will provide plenty more protection to you. Remove the nails with out damaging the wood by means of using way of cautiously the use of a claw hammer, pry bar, or a cat's paw (which looks as If a small pry bar). Needle-nostril pliers can also are available to be had alongside facet the aforementioned gear if the nails are deeply embedded or rusty.

Feed the Saw

If you are familiar with the stitching tool, which you want to feed the fabric to it. The identical applies to woodwork. Never pressure the timber into the discovered; it's miles hazardous as it may ward off the wood, ensuing in harm. Be affected person and feed the timber to the noticed; permit the noticed do its artwork. Every newbie wishes to learn how to paintings in the direction of the lowering device on this way, bringing the wooden into the table sure blade.

Single Cords

Many humans are accountable of getting many cords which may be knotted or get pulled out whilst we artwork. Especially in case you take 1/2-hour to recognize that your cord pulled out and not whatever is inaccurate at the side of your equipment! You've in all likelihood observed out they are dropping present day, no longer to say posing a protection hazard with a knot of interwoven cables. They additionally will be inclined to disrupt art work on every occasion one or more connections turn out to be unfastened.

Develop a addiction to continually hire a unmarried extension cable whilst using electricity gadget over a larger distance than their associated twine lets in. Moreover, make sincerely certain you are the use of a sturdy enough cable to offer desirable sufficient strength over an extended distance. You'll be doing extra stable and in addition precise work with out the threat of having many electricity equipment or saws walking on the same time and competing for strength with every extraordinary.

Reaching Over Blades

Another mistake frequently made thru way of these the usage of woodworking device with taking walks blades is to try to achieve, or lean, over the blade even as it's though grew to turn out to be on. You always want to bear in thoughts to every gain round it slowly or turn the tool off altogether. By leaning over a blade, you could in all likelihood lose your stability and end up entering into contact with the blade; this could probably cause a severe emergency, in all likelihood even inflicting everlasting accidents or deadly ones.

You also can make use of a blade defend to be nice you'll be steady from the pointy blade. Leave the blade shield on as masses as feasible whilst walking; and, use warning while disposing of a shield, making sure the blade is grew to grow to be off. You'll have a blade come to be pinched every so often, wherein the blade turns into stuck in a chunk of wooden on the identical time as reducing. Definitely be sure that there can be no energy to the blade earlier than you try and dislodge it, moving the wood to remove the pinch factor so that you can without trouble eliminate the noticed.

Distractions and Help

Interruptions divert your interest and recognition far from the mission handy. When you're the use of powerful or sharp gear, any distraction that attracts your thoughts faraway from what you're doing can bring about an twist of fate occurring in a fragment of a minute. If the mobile phone earrings, there may be a noisy noise outdoor, or someone walks into your artwork vicinity, you can turn out to be distracted inside the blink of an eye. You can reduce some interruptions through leaving your cell telephone in every other room or setting a Do Not Disturb join up your workshop door, however it's in reality now not possible to remove all resources which can divert your hobby. Always supply attention to what you're doing and don't artwork while you're worn-out, so you can preserve manipulate of the device you're the usage of regardless of what goes on spherical you.

Clamping Work Pieces

Woodwork substances that are unfastened and risky might be risky. A clamp is a fastening mechanism that makes use of inward stress to maintain or normal matters carefully collectively to restrict motion or separation. If the materials you're the usage of are not secured and loose, they may be inadvertedly flung off the working floor or spin brief—both of which may be volatile!

Read and Think!

When have come to be the final time you read the guide after shopping or selecting a today's device? Are you this kind of folks that in reality toss the instructions aside and start placing collectively and the use of your new buy? Besides safety information, customer manuals include masses of suggestions and facts that allow you to get the most out of the product you're the usage of. Whether you're a woodworking amateur or surely the utilization of new tools, make certain to take a look at the instructions; and, if there's something you don't understand, you could regularly discover tutorials to examine on YouTube.

Ask for Help

There's no disgrace in soliciting for help. Whether you need extra manpower to maintain down or bring an object, or need a few issue described to you in greater element (or in a way you can understand it better), ask an professional wood employee for assist!

Shop Safety

Everyone who enters your woodworking workshop need to be careful to keep the workspace and placed on appropriate garb and footwear. Cleaning up after a mission is an crucial part of keeping a strong workshop. Clutter and debris can't first-rate restrict you timewise, but is probably unstable. A artwork-free vicinity of the store can be used for exciting, retaining rings and one in all a type gadgets, or likely ingesting a snack or ingesting a soda or espresso. Lockers are some specific possibility for storing belongings that you need to hold a short distance away however in which they won't intrude along with your art work. Building shelves and hangers to hold tools and other materials keeps them off the ground and from your way in the paintings place, as long as they're sturdy enough to keep what you vicinity on them. Have you heard the time period "clean bench?" This policy, if you decide to position it in area, approach that you may pass back all substances and equipment to their rightful region after completing a challenge. Wearing a toolbelt can keep you from continuously searching out nails, screws, and so on. Ensure that there are sufficient shops to your electricity machine and device for the duration of the workshop so you gained't need to plug in a few aspect and then run the wire to the opportunity factor of the room. This prevents tripping and unintentional disconnects.

If you've ever owned a swimming pool, then you definately're probably conscious that a few chemical substances must be stored an extended manner from each particular or from gasoline because of the fact they may be combustible. This applies to 3 substances on your workshop that need to be saved separately and segregated in garage. Heavy items should be stored at a pinnacle that is identical to the region above the knee however lower than your shoulders to prevent bending or attaining too a protracted manner while moving or lifting heavy or awkward gadgets. Keep those gadgets upright.

Be superb all bottles or boxes are classified, and that you may in reality have a look at it. Do not maintain chemical substances in meals containers. Dispose of sharp, pointed items and broken glass in a bin with a marked contend with product of metal or robust plastic to save you punctures. Things in garage should be inspected regularly to make sure they will be even though needed, and previous gadgets must be discarded.

Smoke and carbon dioxide detectors want to be installation in your shop. A fireplace extinguisher is also a want. I propose maintaining a flashlight inside acquire in case the lighting fixtures exit. This is, thru a long way, masses a great deal much less expensive than installing emergency lighting.

Dust Collection and Ventilation

Let's speak about dirt: it's now not definitely turning on a vacuum and sucking up the dust. Unfortunately, there may be a outstanding deal greater to outstanding dust manipulate in a woodshop. You're probable thinking, "Why problem?"

No rely how an awful lot you vacuum and how frequently you use a Shop-Vac, there'll continuously be dust everywhere at the ground of your workspace, your system, or maybe inside the car. You can trust the effects that every one those high-quality debris can also need to your sinuses! You're no longer by myself if any of it resonates with you. For most woodworkers, it's miles a situation they've got encountered at some time.

Gathering and putting off dust is vital for defensive your self from inhalation of chemicals, as well as preventing fires. Machines function better whilst no airborne particles are clogging up the gears. Working in a easy surroundings is likewise higher to your mood and for buying responsibilities finished correctly.

Wood dust consists of chemicals and micro organism that, thru inhalation over the years, can motive or make worse first-rate ailments. Some of these include breathing conditions (e.G., allergies, bronchitis, and so forth.); malignancies of the nostril, throat, and lung; continual obstructive pulmonary ailment (COPD); and acute allergic reactions. Being allergic to dust impairs your capability to complete tasks in a nicely timed manner, because of all the eye itchiness and functionality sneezing. Accumulation of dust can intervene with the precision of workshop device and require greater maintenance on gadget.

Fire! Tools which include routers and sanders can produce hundreds of timber dust, or sawdust. These first-rate particulates are far greater combustible and burn hundreds a whole lot much less difficult than whole pieces of lumber. Dust can acquire speedy in corners, on rafters, and plenty of others. If thorough cleanup isn't completed. All you need to do is take a step-stool or ladder to get to a higher shelf and blow in some unspecified time in the future of the shelf to look how a bargain dirt has quietly accumulated with out you even know-how it.

Chapter 7: Essential Tools for a Beginner

"What gadget do I need? Will or now not it's miles highly-priced? Will I be capable of control

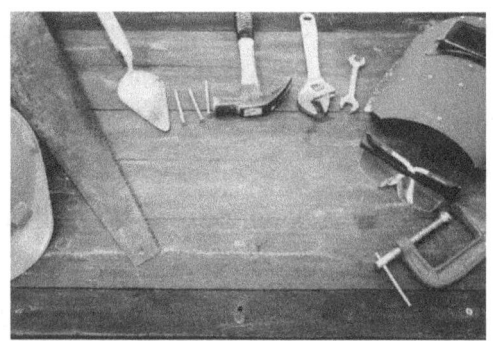

to pay for it?"

Despite what some human beings declare, device do play a huge role in determining a craftsman's fulfillment. The appropriate collection of primary woodworking gear for novices can't simplest growth your revel in with the trade but can even save you loads of coins within the long term. None of the costly tool that might occupy a -automobile garage is protected. For starters and intermediate woodworkers, this ebook concentrates on the fundamentals.

To begin a profession in woodworking, you do now not want to spend a number of money. Investing only a few hundred greenbacks in exceptional tools can also furthermore get you up and on foot proper away. I'm going to give you a list of the pleasant startup hand and small energy equipment that you'll want, and also you gained't recollect the subjects which you could have already got at your fingertips. Pencils for marking are in all likelihood mendacity spherical your property somewhere, and who doesn't have a tape degree hiding in a drawer?

Woodworking merchandise which may be vital for novices:

• a measuring device

• squares

• clamps

• hand noticed

• aircraft

• claw hammer

- a mallet and set of chisels

- stones for sharpening

- spherical noticed

- router

- energy drill

- orbital sander

- jigsaw

- pencils

- workbench

Measurements will appear like a monster. When going through measurements, you can become panicky and worried you would possibly lessen to rubble the size if you need to price you your undertaking, but don't worry! You don't want to be a genius for this; all you need to do is ensure your measurements are accurate! Some humans truely lessen, degree, and decrease another time;but, if you were to reduce more than you must, you'll possibly want to start at some stage in! That's why you have to continually double-take a look at your measurements in advance than you chop—as a end result the pronouncing: Measure instances, reduce as quickly as.

Without measurements, many elements of the wooden will no longer be accurate. The period, depth, weight, and so on., are all laid low with measurements. So, make certain to do it nicely. Don't worry; you've had been given this and I'm here to manual you.

A Measuring Device

Speaking of monster measurements, the number one device you want is a measuring tool. A measuring device performs an important thing in ensuring your woodwork is designed efficiently. Just guessing wherein to reduce and grind will honestly assist you grow to be with a unique piece at the end, but I'm assuming you want it to be practical, as well, and a few aspect you are proud to show to others.

What Kinds of Measurement Tools Do You Need?

There are loads of devices that can be applied in measuring and marking. Pencils are great for marking on timber and one-of-a-kind surfaces, and I'll bet you have got got got a few mendacity around the residence? If no longer, then select out out up a tough and speedy of extremely good ones. While you're at it, let's ensure you have a marking knife, a measuring tape that has each metric and desired measurements on it (e.G., centimeters and inches, and lots of others.), a six to twelve inch ruler (or a folding rule, which suits to your pocket), and probable even a marking gauge. What Is Each Used For?

Even if you have a energy lowering tool that has a laser beam, as a few more moderen ones do, you'll nonetheless want to mark your wooden with a pencil earlier than decreasing. Why do you want a marking knife, too? The motive is that, no matter the truth that you'll maximum in all likelihood use pencils maximum of the time, there are times in which you're going to want a completely unique cut and the pencil mark is probably a bit hard to appearance; or, you need to mark the spot with a marking (or setting) knife so you have a place to start your chisel or noticed, putting it slightly into the carved mark.

Measuring tapes are so small, however can be pulled out pretty a distance or perhaps locked in region, that's notable in case you're on foot by myself. Make sure it has measurements in each vast and metric, so that it obtained't take into account if the commands you examine say six centimeters or six inches—you'll be prepared for each one. Twenty-five toes might be the length of a top notch-sized measuring tape, and it's miles very clean to hold the tape and produce it with you quite an entire lot anywhere. You may moreover even convey it with you in your device belt with the assist of a belt loop attachment. This will permit for fast measuring at your fingertips. The simplest assets you want to do are stretch the tape out, positioned it near the object you would like to diploma, and placed the lock in region. Tape measures sometimes include a button with a purpose to fast retract the tape as quickly as you have got completed measuring, irrespective of the fact that a few will retract through themselves as speedy because the lock is taken off.

A reasonably-priced ruler is notable on the identical time as laying out joists, and so forth. A folding rule is available, too due to its compact duration whilst folded. It's what humans used in advance than the tape diploma, and most (like myself) in spite of the fact that use them now and again.

With the marking gauge, you could lock a size in area on the tool to apply again and again in great spots. These are clean to use for any woodwork level, and are vital whilst fixtures making. They're furthermore mainly crucial for the joinery in woodwork, due to the fact the measurement desires to be specific. There are even wheel decreasing marking gauges. Be careful while buying a marking gauge, due to the reality a number of those to be had are very low fine. Get yourself both an high-quality wood cutting (or reducing) gauge or a wheel gauge. A cutting gauge will slice in some unspecified time in the future of the grain in a crisp, particular mark. My favored, a wheel cutter gauge, has a cutter blade on it that is spherical and creates a super, real mark.

Squares

For the ones just starting in woodworking, aggregate squares are a need to-have. This is a length device with immediately edges. The aggregate rectangular's simplicity of use and adaptableness make it an amazing option above terrific squares. Other accessible squares are the framing rectangular, the try square, pace rectangular (rafter rectangular), and double rectangular. The very last is just like a combination square, but first-class measures at a 90 diploma attitude at the same time as a aggregate may even artwork for forty five diploma angles. Although attempt squares are smooth to use, I've observed firsthand that many are out of square while you first get them, and are hard to preserve in square. Getting them again in square can be time ingesting, using a record and a board. A framing square, or carpenter's square, is used without a doubt as you'd bet through it's name—for laying out frames, roofing rafters, and stairs. It was formerly known as a metallic square. A pace square is well-known as it's compact in period and might do numerous subjects, which includes marking any thoughts-set from 0 stages to 90 stages.

How and Why Do You Benefit From Owning a Combination Square?

A first rate mixture rectangular is essential in the equal way that a marking gauge is; it is an vital woodworking device for beginners as it lets in create exquisite angles. For woodworking, the ones are the 2 maximum huge angles: ninety and forty five degrees. Making mortise and tenon connections, as an instance, necessitate unique ninety-diploma angles whilst reducing a board to length or attaching the edges of boards. This device is crucial no matter whether or not or no longer you advocate to apply power tools. Due to its many features, which incorporates being useful for leveling and measuring (collectively with the aforementioned marking), it could simply do the task of numerous different system.

Which One to Purchase?

Thinking approximately mixture squares, you'll mechanically expect they'll be one-hundred percentage 90 stages, however it is no longer always the case. Some aggregate squares may be off through using some stages, that can reduce to rubble your measurements on the prevent whilst assembling the item, even though it is without a doubt via one degree. It can degree the center of round devices, to determine the intensity of an item, and to show the customer at the same time as some component is level via the usage of the bubble lever that most combination squares have on them. The twelve inch square is the maximum famous due to the fact it is able to be the most useful to your woodworking keep due to its versatility, however a four or six inch one may be handier because it's greater compact and you may toss it in your pocket, tool belt, or apron.

Would you obtain as proper with that the principle reason lots of folks that experience operating with wooden choose out the combination rectangular over precise sorts of squares is due to the manner it suits on your hand? It's like a one-duration-fits-all, fine (no longer like garb) it without a doubt does in shape all! Because you could with out trouble preserve close to it and maintain it in opposition to the piece you're strolling on, you haven't any want to over-amplify your hand whether or not or not your hand is massive or small.

The aggregate square you purchase want to stay rectangular or your measurements may be off and, regardless of the truth that mild-weight aluminum works superb on the begin, it can short turn out to be warped from repeated use. You will maximum in all likelihood select the weighty experience of one with a cast-iron inventory. Just remember the antique adage: You get what you pay for. If you discover a truly reasonably-priced one, it'll possibly lack a top notch deal of the accuracy you'll want.

Clamps

Woodworkers can't do with out clamps. Any wood worker will assist you to understand that there may be no such thing as too many, and having a collection of clamps can be useful! Those who've been taking component in their woodworking journey for years will likely have a huge form of clamps of their workshop, due to the fact you can use them for such severa topics! You can use them to maintain your paintings quantities together whilst the glue is drying, or to quick fasten the timber to the desk in a strong position in order that it received't drift while sawing or strolling at the complicated records of your masterpiece.

Why You'll Want to Use Them

As stated above, there are a plethora of uses for clamps. By fastening the object of your attention in vicinity, you're loose to paintings on it with out worrying approximately it transferring or slipping, which could harm your hard art work. Clamps are vital for pretty some reasons, mainly in woodworking. They can be used to preserve longer boards desk bound, as a spreader to push two pieces apart, for utilising finishing touches, and lots of others.

The opportunities are infinite and there are even net websites with hacks to apply special clamps mixed with precise equipment to create a completely unique clamp for nearly whatever. The severa styles of clamps used even as crafting with timber encompass C-clamps, F-clamps, bar clamps, pipe clamps, bench clamps, strap clamps, spring clamps, handscrew clamps, and so forth.